PERSIAN GULF WAR: AN ASSESSMENT OF HEALTH OUTCOMES ON THE 25TH ANNIVERSARY

HEARING

BEFORE THE

SUBCOMMITTEE ON OVERSIGHT AND INVESTIGATIONS

OF THE

COMMITTEE ON VETERANS' AFFAIRS U.S. HOUSE OF REPRESENTATIVES

ONE HUNDRED FOURTEENTH CONGRESS

SECOND SESSION

TUESDAY, FEBRUARY 23, 2016

Serial No. 114–57

Printed for the use of the Committee on Veterans' Affairs

Available via the World Wide Web: http://www.fdsys.gov

U.S. GOVERNMENT PUBLISHING OFFICE

25–103   WASHINGTON : 2017

COMMITTEE ON VETERANS' AFFAIRS

JEFF MILLER, Florida, *Chairman*

DOUG LAMBORN, Colorado
GUS M. BILIRAKIS, Florida, *Vice-Chairman*
DAVID P. ROE, Tennessee
DAN BENISHEK, Michigan
TIM HUELSKAMP, Kansas
MIKE COFFMAN, Colorado
BRAD R. WENSTRUP, Ohio
JACKIE WALORSKI, Indiana
RALPH ABRAHAM, Louisiana
LEE ZELDIN, New York
RYAN COSTELLO, Pennsylvania
AMATA COLEMAN RADEWAGEN, American
  Samoa
MIKE BOST, Illinois

CORRINE BROWN, Florida, *Ranking
  Minority Member*
MARK TAKANO, California
JULIA BROWNLEY, California
DINA TITUS, Nevada
RAUL RUIZ, California
ANN M. KUSTER, New Hampshire
BETO O'ROURKE, Texas
KATHLEEN RICE, New York
TIMOTHY J. WALZ, Minnesota
JERRY McNERNEY, California

JON TOWERS, *Staff Director*
DON PHILLIPS, *Democratic Staff Director*

SUBCOMMITTEE ON OVERSIGHT AND INVESTIGATION

MIKE COFFMAN, Colorado, *Chairman*

DOUG LAMBORN, Colorado
DAVID P. ROE, Tennessee
DAN BENISHEK, Michigan
TIM HUELSKAMP, Kansas
JACKIE WALORSKI, Indiana

ANN M. KUSTER, New Hampshire, *Ranking
  Member*
BETO O'ROURKE, Texas
KATHLEEN RICE, New York
TIMOTHY J. WALZ, Minnesota

CONTENTS

Tuesday, February 23, 2016

Page

Persian Gulf War: An Assessment of Health Outcomes on the 25th Anniversary 1

OPENING STATEMENTS

Honorable Mike Coffman, Chairman 1
Honorable Ann M. Kuster, Ranking Member 2

WITNESSES

Carolyn Clancy, M.D., Deputy Under Secretary for Health for Organizational Excellence, U.S. Department of Veterans Affairs 4
    Accompanied by:
      Stephen Hunt, M.D., M.P.H., Director, Post-Deployment Integrated Care Initiative, U.S. Department of Veterans Affairs
      Victor Kalasinsky, Ph.D., Senior Program Manager, Gulf War Veterans' Illnesses Research, U.S. Department of Veterans Affairs
Deborah Cory-Slechta, Ph.D., Professor of Environmental Medicine, Pediatrics and Public Health Sciences, Acting Chair, Department of Environmental Medicine, University of Rochester School of Medicine 6
    Prepared Statement 27
Roberta F. White, Ph.D., Chair, Department of Environmental Health, Boston University School of Public Health 9
    Prepared Statement 30
    Accompanied by:
      Mr. James H. Binns, Gulf War Researcher, Former Chairman, Research Advisory Committee on Gulf War Veterans' Illnesses
Mr. Anthony Hardie, Gulf War Veteran, Director, Veterans for Common Sense 10
    Prepared Statement 33
    Accompanied by:
    Mr. David K. Winnett, II, Gulf War Veteran

STATEMENTS FOR THE RECORD

Lung Cancer Alliance 38
National Gulf War Resource Center 39
Mr. James H. Binns 41
Ms. Montra Denise Nichols, MSN 69
Kimberly Sullivan, PhD 73
Mr. David K. Winnett, II 75
Lea Steele, Ph.D. 81

QUESTIONS FOR THE RECORD

Questions from Chairman Mike Coffman for the Department of Veterans Affairs: 83

PERSIAN GULF WAR: AN ASSESSMENT OF HEALTH OUTCOMES ON THE 25TH ANNIVERSARY

Tuesday, February 23, 2016

U.S. HOUSE OF REPRESENTATIVES,
COMMITTEE ON VETERANS' AFFAIRS,
SUBCOMMITTEE ON OVERSIGHT
AND INVESTIGATIONS,
Washington, D.C.

The Subcommittee met, pursuant to notice, at 4:35 p.m., in Room 334, Cannon House Office Building, Hon. Mike Coffman [Chairman of the Subcommittee] presiding.

Present: Representatives Coffman, Roe, Huelskamp, Kuster, and Walz.

Also Present: Representative Denham.

OPENING STATEMENT OF MIKE COFFMAN, CHAIRMAN

Mr. COFFMAN. Good afternoon. This hearing will come to order. I want to welcome everybody to today's hearing entitled "Persian Gulf War: An Assessment of Health Outcomes on the 25th Anniversary."

First, as a preliminary matter, I would like to ask unanimous consent that—let's see. Who do we have? Oh, I guess they're not here. I don't have to do that.

Ms. KUSTER. The answer is yes.

Mr. COFFMAN. As a fellow Gulf War veteran, I have invited them. Unfortunately, they're not here. Let's see.

This hearing will examine VA's treatment of and current health outcomes for veterans suffering from Gulf War illness. The hearing will focus largely on the issues that have arisen since our last hearing on Gulf War illness on March 13, 2013, and specifically review VA's efforts to improve treatment and outcomes. This hearing marks the 25th anniversary of the Persian Gulf War, a conflict of swift intensity and short duration with what could be the lowest incident of post-traumatic stress disorder of any American war, according to some reports, including VA's own National Center for Post-Traumatic Stress Disorder.

Unfortunately, this anniversary also marks numerous problems, some of which haven't improved since our hearing on Gulf War illness 3 years ago. I'm deeply concerned about how VA continues to characterize Gulf War illness as a mental disorder, as evident in its current clinical guidelines. I'm perplexed that these same clinical guidelines are based in part on research that the Institute of

Medicine has warned is potentially biased or influenced by pharmaceutical manufacturers. I'm also frustrated by the fact that VA is prescribing psychotropic drugs for not only Gulf War illness but apparently also for instances of traumatic brain injury and post-traumatic stress. And I wonder about a possible connection between drug manufacturers and their sponsored studies and the high rate of prescription drugs being dumped on veterans with Gulf War illness. My concerns regarding VA's overuse of drugs are well founded, given this Committee's hearing last June that revealed VA administrators acknowledging the practice of overprescribing medication and turning veterans into drug addicts.

VA has previously testified that Gulf War illness is not a mental malady. And its own training course states that it, quote, "cannot be ascribed to any known psychiatric disorder, somatoform disorder, PTSD, or depression," unquote. Even so, VA continues to treat veterans as if Gulf War illness was a psychiatric problem. And that is an affront to those who have real physical ailments due to their service.

I find it hard to believe cardiovascular disease, the physical scarring of lungs, central sleep apnea, head trauma, cataracts, and a variety of cancers are the manifestation of psychosomatic or psychiatric issues. If it could be as simple as a veteran thinking such things exist and then they disappear, I would think—simply think—VA is an organization truly capable of caring for veterans, and all of the Department's continued failures would simply be resolved.

What is even more frustrating is that the Institute of Medicine is apparently recommending no more Gulf War illness research be conducted. And that makes no sense whatsoever. But, then again, VA has published so few recent studies that this seems part and parcel of business as usual.

Gulf War veterans, myself among them, are tired of hearing the same rhetoric from the VA. Quite frankly, I have had enough of VA telling me one thing and doing the exact opposite. The fact that very little, if anything, has changed in the 3 years since we last held a hearing on VA's treatment of Gulf War illness is not only completely unacceptable; it is infuriating. I look forward to a spirited discussion on this important issue.

With that, I yield to Ranking Member Kuster for any opening remarks that she may have.

OPENING STATEMENT OF ANN M. KUSTER, RANKING MEMBER

Ms. KUSTER. Thank you, Chairman Coffman.

And thank you for your service in the Gulf War. We're all grateful for that.

Sunday marks the 25th anniversary of the end of Operation Desert Storm. And over the course of this quarter century, many veterans who served in that conflict have suffered from symptoms that are not readily identifiable or well understood. In fact, nearly 30 percent of Gulf War veterans suffer from Gulf War illness. These veterans still struggle to receive accurate diagnoses for their symptoms and access to needed health care. These veterans struggle to get effective treatment for their conditions. And for too many years, veterans suffering from Gulf War illness have been told: It's all in your head.

I think we can all agree today that Gulf War illness is not psychosomatic. Gulf War illness is a chronic, often painful, and sometimes debilitating disease. And our veterans deserve access to VA care and the most effective treatments for their illnesses and injuries.

I'm concerned that recent findings from the Institute of Medicine may have been interpreted by some to mean that veterans should only receive mental health treatment for Gulf War illness. I'm also concerned that recent research findings may be interpreted to deny Gulf War veterans and all veterans suffering from ill-defined conditions access to VA health care and effective treatments.

I wish to hear from all of our witnesses today so that we may begin to better understand the conclusions and recommendations of the researchers and experts in this field. It's so very important that we develop clear goals to ensure that our veterans receive access to health care, both for mental health and physical health symptoms, and the most effective treatment for their service-connected injuries and illnesses.

We know that veterans of the Iraq and Afghanistan wars are also coming to VA hospitals in need of treatment for their symptoms, sometimes symptoms that are similar to those suffered by Gulf War veterans. That's why it's vital that the research continues so that we will best understand the very best treatments and continue to explore issues relating to causation in order to protect the health of our servicemembers going forward. I believe it's incumbent upon us to learn as much as we can about what are our Nation is asking from our servicemembers and their families when they volunteer and raise their right hand. We must recognize and be prepared to address the cost of that service and use our best efforts to ensure that our veterans are made whole again after returning home.

And here I might just add that the Chairman and I spent time together over Thanksgiving in Afghanistan. And one of the concerns is, if we don't understand the causation behind the Gulf War syndrome and exposure to toxins or other trauma, psychological injury, PTSD, TBI, and how this is all coming together, we're not going to have an understanding of what it means to put our current troops in harm's way in Iraq and Afghanistan. So I feel very strongly that we need to continue to investigate causation while we move forward with treatment for veterans that have already been exposed.

So thank you, and I yield back.

Mr. COFFMAN. Thank you, Ranking Member Kuster.

We are now joined by United States Representative Jeff Denham from the State of California, a Gulf War veteran.

I ask unanimous approval for Mr. Denham to be able to participate in this hearing.

Ms. KUSTER. Absolutely.

Welcome, Mr. Denham.

Mr. COFFMAN. So ordered.

Mr. DENHAM. I get my own card.

Mr. COFFMAN. Thank you, Ranking Member Kuster.

I ask that all Members waive their openings remarks as per this Committee's custom.

With that, I invite the first and only panel to the witness table. You are currently seated. On that panel, for the Department of Veterans Affairs, we have Dr. Carolyn Clancy, Deputy Under Secretary for Health for Organizational Excellence. She is accompanied by Dr. Stephen Hunt, Director of VA's Post-Deployment Integrated Care Initiative, U.S. Department of Veterans Affairs, and Dr. Victor Kalasinsky—I believe, got that wrong—senior program manager for VA's Gulf War Veterans' Illnesses Research, VA.

Also on the panel, we have Dr. Deborah Cory-Slechta, Professor of Environmental Medicine, Pediatrics and Public Health Sciences, and Acting Chair of the Department of Environmental Medicine at the University of Rochester School of Medicine, who will be testifying in her capacity as chair on the Committee on Gulf War and Health of the Institute of Medicine.

Dr. Roberta F. White, chair of the Department of Environmental Health at Boston University School of Public Health, who is accompanied by Mr. James H. Binns, Gulf War Researcher and former chairman of the Research Advisory Committee on Gulf War Veterans' Illnesses.

And Mr. Anthony Hardie, a Gulf War veteran and Director of Veterans for Common Sense, who is accompanied by Mr. David K. Winnett, II, a Gulf War veteran.

I ask the witnesses to please stand and raise your right hand. [Witnesses sworn.]

Mr. COFFMAN. Very well. Sit down. Please be seated. And let the record reflect that all witnesses have answered in the affirmative.

Dr. Clancy, you are now recognized for 5 minutes.

STATEMENT OF CAROLYN CLANCY, M.D.

Dr. CLANCY. Thank you. Good afternoon, Chairman Coffman, Ranking Member Kuster, Members of the Subcommittee, Representative Denham. I'm accompanied today by Dr. Stephen Hunt, director of our Post-Deployment Integrated Care Initiative. As Deputy Under Secretary for Organizational Excellence and an internist, my background has been conducting and supporting research to improve patient care and inform public policy for much of my career. So I know how important it is to get the science right and assure you that VA is taking every step possible to advance research, clinical care, and education on Gulf War illness.

Since our last hearing in 2013, VA has funded or conducted over 60 studies. Funding for Gulf War research has increased steadily from $5.6 million in 2011 to over $14 million this year. And that's a very conservative estimate. For example, a study funded this past June is a randomized trial of something called CoQ10 thought to change subcellular function in a way that could help treat the effects of Gulf War illness. Other studies evaluate the effectiveness of a broad range of treatments for musculoskeletal pain, fatigue, and cognitive issues using exercise programs, magnetic stimulation, and other innovative approaches. So, as we look for promising interventions through research, VA is also working diligently to treat these veterans that are now suffering from Gulf War illness.

From 2000 to 2015 the percentage of Gulf War veterans enrolled in our system has increased from 13 percent to about 33 percent. We offer continuing evaluation and treatment to the over 700,000 men and women who served in Operations Desert Shield and Desert Storm. We have centers of excellence, three of them, called War Related Injury and Illness Study Centers, or WRIISCs—and we want to express our appreciation to the Congress for these— which are charged with conducting cutting-edge research, clinical education, and providing specialized care for Gulf War veterans with complex chronic unexplained or very difficult-to-diagnosis conditions. And demand for their services is no surprise; as the number of Gulf War veterans has increased, demand for these services has also increased.

In addition, a total of 145,000 Gulf War veterans have undergone a Gulf War registry exam allowing their health concerns to be evaluated by VA physicians and enabling them to be referred for additional care. We first learned from Gulf War veterans just how important it is to integrate all the care and services that veterans need, and to integrate and organize that around the veteran and the veteran's needs. And, in fact, that became an organizing principle for much of our system and team-based primary care. And, in fact, that has helped us to organize our referrals to community providers when necessary as well.

We know that many Gulf War veterans are affected by a debilitating cluster of medically unexplained chronic symptoms that can include fatigue, headaches, joint pain, indigestion, insomnia, dizziness, respiratory disease, memory problems. And the chronic multisymptom illness we see so often in Gulf War veterans is clearly not a psychological condition. So I want to be very clear on that. We're committed to ensuring our research, clinical care, and education takes into account all of the factors that are relevant to returning that veteran to the highest level of function. We have aggressively pursued and fast-tracked studies in ways we can meet the research and treatment needs for all veterans that have been affected by environmental exposures. So that research serves two purposes. One is to improve clinical care that we're providing now for those enrolled in our system. And the other is as the basis for presumptions or other benefits. Our philosophy has been to come down on the side of the veteran when the science supports it. And, as you've seen, we have made our policies more liberal for C123 crews and are now adding new presumptives for veterans who served at Camp Lejeune. In addition, we've been working with Ron Brown at the National Gulf War Resource Center to address a number of concerns and possible presumptions for Gulf War veterans.

Going forward, we recognize that while we've learned a lot, we need and value the ongoing feedback and input from our stakeholders, this committee of course, the Research Advisory Committee, the Veterans Service Organizations, and, very importantly, Gulf War veterans themselves.

As we conduct an in-depth review of the most recent Institute of Medicine report, we're going to include 2 full days to receive public comments and feedback from our stakeholders and partners to assure that VA's priorities are informed by veterans and stakeholders.

You know, vigorous disagreements in science are part of the landscape, and we welcome that at all times. That's what moves science forward. And we're committed to hearing from all sides.

That concludes my testimony. My colleague and I look forward to answering your questions that you or the Committee may have.

[THE PREPARED STATEMENT OF CAROLYN CLANCY, M.D. APPEARS IN THE APPENDIX]

Mr. COFFMAN. Thank you, Dr. Clancy.

Dr. Cory-Slechta, you are now recognized for 5 minutes.

STATEMENT OF DEBORAH CORY-SLECHTA, PH.D.

Ms. CORY-SLECHTA. Good afternoon. Is this on?

I am Deborah Cory-Slechta, professor of environmental medicine, pediatrics, and public health sciences, and acting chair of the Department of Environmental Medicine at the University of Rochester School of Medicine. I served as chair of the "Committee on Gulf War and Health, Volume 10," which was released February 11 of this year. The committee that I was chaired was asked to review and evaluate the scientific and medical literature regarding associations between illness and exposure to toxic agents, environmental or wartime hazards, or preventative medicines or vaccines associated with Gulf War service, paying particular attention to neurological disorders, including Parkinson's, MS, ALS, and migraines, to cancer, particularly brain cancer and lung cancer, and chronic multisymptom illness, also known as Gulf War illness. Volume 10 updates two earlier Gulf War and Health reports: volume 4, in 2006, and volume 8, that was published in 2010.

The committee made recommendations for future research on Gulf War veterans. And I would note that this committee was composed of experts in neurology, epidemiology, pain, psychiatry, neurocognitive disorders, environmental health, and toxicology. And they were clinicians and researchers, none of whom received funding from Gulf War illness research programs.

Volume 10 basically followed the approach used by earlier committees. We held two public sessions at which we heard from representatives of the VA, from Gulf War veterans, and Veterans Service Organizations, Gulf War researchers, and representatives of the VA Research Advisory Committee. We did not address policy issues such as service-connection, compensation or the cause of or treatment for Gulf War illness. We conducted an extensive literature search, reviewed the volumes 4 and 8 conclusions, as well as their primary and secondary studies. We also looked at animal toxicology, neuroimaging, and genetics. We tried to be totally inclusive. We divided our studies into primary studies. They had to be published in peer-reviewed journals demanding—or demonstrating reporting rigorous methods, including information on a persistent, not acute, health outcomes, used appropriate laboratory testing as applicable, and had a study population that was generalizable to and representative of the Gulf War population.

Secondary studies were those studies that didn't meet all of these criteria. Many of the secondary studies relied on self-reports of diagnoses rather than examination by a health professional or a medical record review. We used the same categories of association that were used in the previous volumes. I won't go through all those. Suffice it to say, we have a sufficient evidence of a causal relationship, sufficient evidence of an association, limited suggestive evidence of an association, inadequate insufficient evidence or limited suggestive evidence of no association.

The committee found that in spite of many millions of dollars that have been spent on researching the health of Gulf War veterans, there has been little substantial progress in our understanding of their health, particularly of Gulf War illness. The volume 10 committee found little evidence to actually warrant changes to the volume 8 conclusions. We fundamentally agree with the volume 8 conclusions regarding the strength of the associations between deployment to the Gulf War and adverse health outcomes. Veterans who were deployed to the Gulf War have an increased risk for many long-term health conditions with—including PTSD, Gulf War illness, chronic fatigue syndrome, functional GI conditions, generalized anxiety disorder, depression, and substance abuse. And in the testimony that I've provided you, you can see our categories of association with different health effects summarized in box 1.

As requested in its statement of tasks, the committee had additional discussions pertaining to Gulf War illness, specifically neurologic conditions, and lung and brain cancer, as well as Gulf War illness itself. So Gulf War illness, of course, is the signature adverse health outcome of having served in the Persian Gulf. Multiple studies have found that some Gulf War veterans, regardless of their country of origin and their different deployment-related exposures, have persistent debilitating and varying symptoms of Gulf War illness. In spite of over two decades of research to define, diagnose, and treat Gulf War illness, little progress has actually been made in elucidating the pathophysiological mechanisms that underlie it, the exposures that may have caused it, or the treatments that are generally effective for it.

Gulf War illness is not an easily diagnosed condition. The committee concluded it is not a psychosomatic illness, but it does, like almost every disease and disorder that we know of, prevent—present with diverse systems, many of which overlap with other health conditions such as chronic fatigue, neurodegenerative disorders, and musculoskeletal.

The committee concluded that, although the existence of an animal model would be advantageous for identifying and evaluating treatment strategies, we caution that developing an animal model is really precluded by the absence of any objective measures of chemical and nonchemical exposures during Gulf War service, let alone the frequency, duration, or dose of those exposures, or the highly likely interactive effects of multiple exposures, about which we know almost nothing. We found it unlikely that a single definitive causal agent will be identified in the many years—this many years after the war. Furthermore, many of the Gulf War studies have excluded the psychological aspects of the condition with regard to both diagnosis and treatment, although veterans report symptoms, such as chronic pain and sleep disturbances, that may be amenable to psychological therapies alone or in conjunction with other treatments.

We found new—little new information pertaining to MS, Parkinson's, or Alzheimer's disease, or migraines. We did recommend that ALS is the only neurologic disease for which we did find limited suggestive evidence for an association. But because the timeframe has been too short to really look at this, we recommended additional followup for prevalence of ALS in this population.

Similarly, we found evidence for brain cancer to be inadequate, insufficient, and it found—we found no statistically significant increase in the current risk of brain concern in deployed Gulf War veterans compared to nondeployed counterparts. A finding that's actually mirrored in another recent IOM study.

With regard to lung cancer, there—in the 10 to 15 years followup that have been reported may not, again, like ALS, have been adequate—an adequate timeframe to really see whether in fact—

Mr. COFFMAN. Dr. Slechta, I'm going to have to ask you to move along, simply because you're at 7 minutes right now.

Ms. CORY-SLECHTA [continued]. Sorry. Okay.

In conclusion, what is striking about this and prior Gulf War and Health Committee's finding is that—well, I'll just skip to the end.

Let me just quickly go through these.

Recognize the connections and complex relations between brain and physical functioning and do not exclude any aspect of Gulf War illness. With respect to improving its diagnosis and treatment, the Department of Veterans Affairs and Department of Defense should develop a joint and cohesive strategy on incorporating emerging diagnostic technologies, personalized approaches to medical care into sufficiently powered future research to inform the studies. I would also say, in regards to what I heard before, the importance of biomonitoring of exposures before, during, and after military—the involvement in the military is going to be critical to ultimately providing any associations to chemical exposures. There need to be followup for neurodegenerative diseases that have long latencies and are associated with aging, as I mentioned before. And let's see. Without definitive and verifiable individual veteran exposure information, further studies to determine cause and effect relationship between Gulf War chemical exposures and health conditions in Gulf War veterans should not be undertaken. We did come up with a list of outcomes where we believe that there are sufficient data already to suggest an association, that we don't need to do more studies to redemonstrate those, somewhere, 25 years after the war, we're not likely to see anything, and so some of those kinds of health conditions didn't warrant followup, as well as some that we said had a longer latency and still needed to be considered.

And, finally, one other thing was to begin to break out sex-specific and race/ethnicity-specific health information, which may be important not only to understanding different vulnerabilities by sex and race but also in terms of understanding mechanisms and treatment for disease.

Thank you. And I'm sorry for going over time.

[THE PREPARED STATEMENT OF DEBORAH CORY-SLECHTA APPEARS IN THE APPENDIX]

Mr. COFFMAN. Thank you, Dr. Slechta.

Dr. White, you are now recognized for 5 minutes.

STATEMENT OF ROBERTA F. WHITE, PH.D.

Ms. WHITE. Chairman Coffman, Ranking Member Kuster, and Members of the House Veterans Affairs Subcommittee on Oversight and Investigations, it's the 25th anniversary of the Gulf War. Our veterans won this conflict in less than a week. However, concern remains high that the troops who produced this victory are and will remain ill without legitimate acknowledgement of their health problems and associated disabilities and without effective treatment options now or in the future.

Despite decades of scientific evidence to the contrary, the VA and the Institute of Medicine have recently produced documents that minimize the poor health of these veterans by terming their illnesses to be functional, a medical term for psychiatric illness. This injustice is then compounded by a VA treatment guideline that suggests ineffective, unproven, palliative, and potentially harmful treatments for Gulf War illness that focus on psychiatric symptomatology. I speak as a clinician scientist who has worked with ill Gulf War veterans clinically and in research for over 20 years. My work on Gulf War illness is part of a 35-year career in which I have studied the effects of exposures to neurotoxic chemicals in adults and children. For 8 years, until last fall, I served as scientific director of the Research Advisory Committee on Gulf War Veterans' Illnesses. It has been known since a year or two after their return from the Gulf that a subset of Gulf War veterans was experiencing debilitating physical illness. Research beginning at that time and continuing to the present has produced a consensus of scientific knowledge about this illness that I will summarize briefly.

First, dozens of studies in multiple countries reveal that approximately 30 percent of the 1991 Gulf War veteran population suffers from a characteristic pattern of physical health symptoms that we call Gulf War illness. This pattern of health symptoms is not seen in veterans of other conflicts.

Second, this illness is not the result of stress or other psychiatric factors. Rates of post-traumatic stress disorder are typically less than 10 percent. Furthermore, rates of Gulf War illness are not significantly higher in Gulf War veterans with psychiatric diagnoses.

Third, Gulf War illness is associated with exposures to chemicals present in theatre, especially pesticides and pyridostigmine bromide, and possibly nerve gas sarin and particulates from the oil well fires.

Fourth, effective treatments for Gulf War illness and other disorders that are induced by chemical exposures that damage the brain do not exist at present. However, recent research has identified treatment options that target specific nervous system and immunological mechanisms of Gulf War illness. These treatments are now being piloted. Despite these treatment advances, new recommendations for treatment of Gulf War illness from VA emphasize immediate referral for mental health evaluation. In addition, cognitive behavioral therapy is suggested. This is a palliative treatment at best and has been shown to be minimally effective in VA research on Gulf War veterans.

Even worse, the treatment guidelines recommend 11 drugs to treat Gulf War illness, 10 of them psychiatric. All 11 drugs are noted in the guidelines to have significant adverse side effects, including suicidal ideation. And these medications have not been studied with regard to their effectiveness in the treatment of Gulf War illness. The recent volume 10 Institute of Medicine report further contributes to this situation by minimizing the health problems of Gulf War veterans and again placing a psychiatric cast on them. Although the volume 10 IOM report states that the science has not changed since the volume 8 report, its conclusions fly in the face of the scientific consensus on Gulf War illness that I have described. The volume 8 report concluded that Gulf War illness cannot be reliably ascribed to any known psychiatric disorder. The volume 10 report distorts and disavows this conclusion by saying that the illness cannot be fully explained by any psychiatric disorder. Unlike prior reports that support mechanistic scientific research on Gulf War illness, volume 10 suggests that it is time research efforts focus on mind/body connectedness, and that further research to determine the relationships between Gulf War exposures and health conditions in Gulf War veterans should not be undertaken. To recommend stopping research into the mechanisms underlying the disease just as research into these mechanisms has begun to make real progress is shockingly shortsighted. And to suggest that psychiatric research has been neglected could not be further from the truth.

During the first 15 years after the war, Federal Gulf War research focused mainly on psychiatric issues with negative results. It is unthinkable that the scientific progress now being made should be halted by a return to the psychogenic era.

Thank you.

[THE PREPARED STATEMENT OF ROBERTA F. WHITE APPEARS IN THE APPENDIX]

Mr. COFFMAN. Thank you, Dr. White.

Mr. Hardie, you're now recognized for 5 minutes.

STATEMENT OF ANTHONY HARDIE

Mr. HARDIE. Thank you, Mr. Chairman, and Ranking Member and Members of this Committee for your service, for this hearing, and for the opportunity to speak with you today.

This is just a brief overview. There are more details in my written submission. I really hope that you'll take the time to read the few pages of it.

I'm Anthony Hardie, a 1991 Gulf War and Somalia veteran. I'm director of the Veterans for Common Sense, and while I've provided testimony on several occasions, today is especially notable. Exactly 25 years ago tonight, we launched the ground war of Operation Desert Storm and successfully liberated Kuwait. Tonight, I would like to—for us to remember and honor the nearly 300 warriors who made the ultimate sacrifice. I would also like us to remember and honor our Gulf War veterans, including those in this room and watching, and our leaders who led us to decisive military victory.

Our war was relatively short, but you've heard our stories before. And with one-fourth and one-third of us coming home with serious and debilitating health issues now known as Gulf War illness, we faced a new battle: a long war to obtain health care, effective health care, and VA assistance from entrenched government officials who seemed intent on minimization and denial at every turn. Even through to today, the VA describes our toxic wounds as medically unexplained. And, finally, in 1998, we won enactment of two landmark bills for Gulf War veterans to guarantee health care and benefits based on research. Yet from the beginning, VA officials circumvented their implementation that leads us to today.

The Institute of Medicine recently released its final report on the Gulf War and Health series under VA contract as directed by the 1998 legislation. It's highly problematic. As I walked through the airport on my way home from the report's release, the weight of the bag with nearly two decades of these IOM reports was heavy on my shoulder. And I want to show that weight.

My heart was even heavier because their collective weight has added little to nothing for Gulf War veterans. It has not associated any of our exposures with our health issues, and has added little towards the development of effective evidence-based treatments for Gulf War illness. The real weight is being borne by Gulf War illness—Gulf War veterans who are suffering from Gulf War illness. This new report recommends no further research using animal models of Gulf War toxic exposures, which amounts to rolling up the sidewalk on this promising avenue of Gulf War illness research just when it's beginning to unravel the underlying mechanisms of Gulf War illness and point to treatment targets. And these new— and this now affects not just non-VA CDMRP research, but VA research as well. In one section, it points out that the VA hasn't reported critical data, but in other, recommends ending research on a long list of health conditions, despite long histories of them in Gulf War veterans not reported by VA. While acknowledging Gulf War illness is a 1991 Gulf War signature condition, there were no Gulf War illness researchers on this panel. It recommends a shift to brain/body interconnectedness that departs from the scientific opinion that effective treatments, cures, and—it is hoped—preventions can likely be found. Instead, this is more like the 1990s, when VA and DoD officials, some of whom are involved in writing this report, denied Gulf War veterans toxic exposures, denied benefits, and failed to develop treatments or preventions. And now VA and DoD have developed a clinical practice guideline that goes back to the very darkest days of the 1990s, authored by some of these same old names and ideas.

Despite VA public statements to the contrary, including to this Committee, this guide for VA and DoD doctors is filled with references to psychosomatic and somatoform disorders; 52 times, to be exact. Its primary recommendations for Gulf War illness are cognitive behavioral therapy or talk therapy, exercise, and psychotropic drugs. Suicidal ideation is listed in the guide as a notable adverse effect for every single one of those medications at a time when we have a suicide crisis amongst veterans. VA has active Gulf War veteran studies on CBT and exercise, but somehow still recommends them as evidence-based in this definitive guide. Twenty-five years after our war, VA has circumvented most of the aims of the 1998 laws intended to help us. In addition to the above, VA lost its registry—lost its registry—for Gulf War spouses and children; ignored and then gutted the Gulf War Research Advisory committee; misleads Congress in its reports to Congress; found no link between Gulf War exposures in Congress, including in these manuals; identified almost no new presumptives. If we measure VA's success by how it's improved Gulf War veterans health 25 years after the war, VA still has not a single evidence-based treatment for Gulf War illness. Others among us have died of ALS, brain cancer, and suicide. And only since the Congressionally Directed Medical Research Program was enacted through the support of many on this committee has VA even begun to look at developing treatments. And while there is real research progress, most of it is being made outside of and in spite of VA in the CDMRP, thanks to many of your support. Twenty-five years later, one-fourth to one-third of us Gulf War veterans continue to struggle with the health and life effects of Gulf War illness. We must not allow—we must not continue to allow VA and DoD to substitute risk communication for evidence-based health care, psychosomatic drugs for treatment-focused research, spin for substance, or don't look/don't find for the objective collection analysis and reporting of deployment health outcomes. The letter, the spirit, and the intent of the 1998 Persian Gulf War laws that we fought so hard to win have yet to be achieved.

And, again, this is just a brief overview. On this 25th anniversary of the Gulf War, our Gulf War veterans deserve the very best that modern science and the U.S. Government can offer to improve their health and lives.

Mr. Chairman, as one of our Gulf War veterans and Members of this powerful Committee, please join together and with your colleagues on both sides of the aisle and in both Houses and help fix these serious issues once and for all. My fellow Gulf War veteran David Winnett and I look forward to your questions. Thank you, again, for this opportunity.

[THE PREPARED STATEMENT OF ANTHONY HARDIE APPEARS IN THE APPENDIX]

Mr. COFFMAN. Thank you for your testimony, Mr. Hardie.

Mr. Hardie, do you recall—and so when we talk about, first of all, the duration of the war, that there were troops on the ground in August of 1990, and then the fact is that the air campaign, I think, started on January 27; ground war started on February 24. But there was certainly contact prior on the ground side with Iraqi forces. But there was—the term—was it "blow in place"?—I think, is a combat engineering term—and that there were chemical munitions—

Mr. HARDIE. Yes, sir.

Mr. COFFMAN [continued].—that were blown in place that the Department of Defense denied. Do you remember what the name of the location was, primary location was, and the date—

Mr. HARDIE. Yes. Mr. Chairman, it was in early March of 1991, after the end of the war. It was at a place called Khamisiyah, and candidly, it was the only one of the incidents that we Gulf War veterans were ever able to get DoD to admit to. There were many others.

Mr. COFFMAN. But it took how long—it took—was it 5 years? I can't remember. What was the time length that it took? Because there was a coverup, quite frankly.

Mr. HARDIE. Yes.

Mr. COFFMAN. Because there were—the page out of General Schwarzkopf's log was missing on that day. All other records were destroyed intentionally. They said they were—I can't remember—accidentally destroyed. But they were destroyed nonetheless. So there were no fingerprints. And the statement by the Department of Defense was that no U.S. troops were exposed to chemical—to any chemical munitions, chemical weapons. We know that's not true today. Nobody faced disciplinary consequences for lying. And then—and then so the research never took that into account because the Department of Defense denied that. How long did it take the Department of Defense to finally acknowledge that U.S. troops had been exposed?

Mr. HARDIE. Well, Mr. Chairman, my understanding—my recollection that it was about 5 years.

Mr. COFFMAN. About 5 years.

Mr. HARDIE. About 1996. And, again, to emphasize, as you just said, that was one of—that was the only incident that we were successfully able to get DoD to acknowledge. And all that information, that evidence, came from Freedom of Information Act requests from a large number of veteran advocates out there who did an incredible job of digging up and finding out what DoD and VA and the CIA did not want to—

Mr. COFFMAN. What was the name of those pills we had to take?

Mr. HARDIE. Pyridostigmine bromide, sir.

Mr. COFFMAN. And they were not FDA approved. Is that correct?

Mr. HARDIE. That's correct. My understanding, though, is that DoD has recently approved them now for use. And that's extremely concerning, given the health effects that me and the men in my unit had. I can't understand how that's even possible.

Mr. COFFMAN. And what was the purpose? Was that for biological or—

Mr. HARDIE. So, sir, it was an anti-nerve-agent prophylactic—

Mr. COFFMAN [continued]. Nerve agent. Okay.

Mr. HARDIE. It was in order to help to improve the survivability if we were hit with one particular nerve agent. Although now research by Dr. White and others has shown that this drug in combination with other chemicals is extremely problematic and—for health, and causes Gulf War illness-like symptoms in laboratory animals. The kind of research that the IOM report recommends ending.

Mr. COFFMAN. And then Saddam Hussein had blown a lot of the oil wellheads to obscure, I think, his own movement or positions of his troops. And then, of course, through our own bombing efforts probably destroyed the balance to where there were days, I remember a wall of black smoke would be coming at you. And you were literally engulfed in that oil well fire. Smoke emanating from those oil well fires for very long periods of time. Do you feel that that's been adequately researched in terms of what the health effects of that were?

Mr. HARDIE. Mr. Chairman, I don't feel that any of it has been adequately researched. I think the VA has done an atrocious job. I think that many of the—there's a long list of conditions in the 1998 laws that were supposed to be—VA was supposed to contract with IOM for. Many of those were never researched, including low levels of mustard, which we know was in the January 19 plumes drifting over the troops. The studies of sarin failed to connect illness in animals exposed to sarin with human health outcomes. That's extremely problematic. And, of course, these days, we're not putting human beings into a gas chamber exposing them to a deadly nerve agent like sarin. So there's this impossible, impossible standard that has prevented the 1998 laws from ever being achieved. Again, I don't believe any of the substances have been adequately researched or in the right ways.

Mr. COFFMAN. Have you—this is my last question. Have you uncovered at all why the command senior leaders, they chose to destroy those chemical weapons there as opposed to properly dispose of them?

Mr. HARDIE. That's a more complicated question, sir. I don't have—I have my own beliefs. But I don't have a good explanation. I do say that it's extraordinarily disappointing, particularly that those logs—General Schwarzkopf's logs disappeared. I served in an intelligence role in the 1991 Gulf War and kept logs of my own, which have never been able to—have been found. My entire unit's medical records have—I'm sorry. Our medical records disappeared. It took a year for our personnel records to show back up as well. And there were a series of chemical incidents, including one nearby to where I was located, where we were—the messages that I was logging were that chemical warfare agents were detected, were confirmed, were confirmed again, and then suddenly it all went away. And the evidence that Gulf War veterans uncovered through Freedom of Information Act requests showed that over and over and over again, the DoD, the CIA, and the VA have all fought all of that across the board. And what we—and it's very clear to all of us. We came back home sick. Twenty-five years later, we've got a stack of volumes that hasn't helped us. We need to do better.

Mr. COFFMAN. Mr. Hardie, thank you so much for your testimony.

Ms. Kuster, you are now recognized.

Ms. KUSTER. Thank you, Mr. Chair.

And thank you, Mr. Hardie, for your service, and, Dr. White, for your reach, and to the whole panel for being with us today.

I'm just thinking of my own personal experience, not in wartime, but I had an illness that was connected with ingestion of volcanic ash. And I was very sick for a very long time. And so my empathy is with you and the veterans exposed to a substance like that, that you don't know, I learned later that it was really ground glass, and when it gets into your lungs, you do get sick. But it was that same feeling of the cloud coming toward you and the helplessness of not— not being able to protect yourself. So my goal here is two-fold. One is to make sure that we have a sufficient understanding to help the veterans from the Gulf War era. And, number two, and equally importantly for me, that we have an understanding to protect our servicemembers who are currently serving abroad.

And so my question, and I'll just put this out to Mr. Hardie and Dr. White, but if anyone else wants to weigh in, have we—I understand your frustration. And I'm just wondering, have we made any progress? Are there individual instances? Are there anecdotal stories of treatments that have been effective that could be more widely used? Let's start with that.

Mr. HARDIE. Maybe if I go first and then Dr. White will have probably other things to add as well. But so there is hope through the efforts of many here in this room, including, thank you, Dr. Roe and Mr. Walz for your leadership in—with the Congressionally Directed Medical Research Program, and for many of you who have signed on in support of that program. It was created in fiscal year 2006, and has shown great progress. But, again, outside of and in spite of the VA, which is now doing some good things thanks to the work of Dr. Kalasinsky, but has a long, long, long ways to go. About a third of the studies funded through this program are testing actual treatments that might help the health and lives of ill Gulf War veterans. The other two-thirds are studies that are aimed at Gulf War illness' underlying mechanisms. They include critically important animal studies that test exposures and measure health outcomes, again, the kinds of things that are now threatened by this IOM report. They identify treatment targets. They test treatments. There are three that have—three treatments—again, much of this is still in the pipeline, but there are three that have been shown to be effective in limited numbers as well: Coenzyme Q–10, carnosine and acupuncture for pain. I take CoQ10 every day. It helps me in a—it helps me a great deal. It's not a cure, but it certainly makes a difference. I've heard the same from other Gulf War veterans. I'm pleased to hear that now we have this study coming from—that will advance it. But, again, it's not a cure. I take it every day. And I can tell you that we have a long—we have—but we're making the progress now through this program. And we hope that VA would finally get onboard with making the systemic changes that need to happen, including in its badly broken Office of Public Health.

Ms. KUSTER. So one of the things we're going to be doing a hearing, a regional hearing, of this Subcommittee actually coming to New Hampshire to talk about opiate use and some interesting research that's going on in White River Junction VA, to bring down the use of opiates using alternative remedies, acupuncture, mindfulness, some of the things that you've mentioned, because I do believe in that mind/body connection. And I don't mean to diminish anything about it. I know that there's certainly illnesses, thyroid illnesses, that type of thing, where it is so closely connected. So I think it's worth exploring these other treatments. And I guess—and because I agree with you that just throwing pills at it, throwing, you know, psychotropic medication that have these down sides with certainly suicidal ideation, et cetera. But just going forward, I'd love to talk with you all about—we're going to be looking hopefully at legislation about best practices in the VA on pain management. Maybe there's a way to bring in some of this research that has gone forward.

And I'd just—Dr. White, I have a very brief time left, but if you have any comments.

Ms. WHITE. I would say that there's a number of lines of treatment approaches that have been supported by CDMRP and more recently VA through our recommendations and work with them on the Research Advisory Committee. Some are aimed at symptoms, brain activation, improving general health and wellbeing. Obviously, when chemicals affect the brain, they affect how you feel as well as how you think and your immune system. And it is a whole body thing. I think what we're trying to say is that there is physical damage to the brain that is causing emotional as well as cognitive and other symptoms. And you need to approach the whole package. One thing that I think is really wonderful about the support we have gotten for the CDMRP programs, and I'm on the integration panel for that, is that we are now working on therapies and trying to fund therapies that get to the neuro-inflammatory and mitochondrial basis of this disease. If we can find treatments that go after the neuro-inflammation, that go after the mitochondrial damage, that go after some of the mechanistisms underlying pathophysiology of this illness, we will not only help the Gulf War veterans, we'll help other people with exposures in the whole world. And these kinds of chemical exposures are very hard to treat, as you know from your own illness. So I think that there's so much promise in the mechanistic-based treatment, as well as the symptomatically focused treatment. I would hate to see that lost. We're finally getting to mechanism. And we were not anywhere close to that 10 years ago.

Ms. KUSTER. No, and I need to yield back. But I agree. And the other half of my question, I—we won't get into it here, but I am extremely concerned that we get upstream on understanding the exposure, because, obviously, you know, I don't have to tell my colleagues that war is a dirty business. But at least we can do our best to protect our troops from smoke and inhalation and that toxic exposure.

So, thank you, Mr. Chairman, for your indulgence.

Mr. COFFMAN. Thank you, Ranking Member Kuster.

Dr. Roe, you're now recognized for 5 minutes.

Mr. ROE. Thank you, Mr. Chairman. And for the group here, I don't know whether you know or not, but I've sponsored a bill called the Desert Storm and Desert Shield War Memorial Act. And we're in the process of—hopefully I'm meeting with Scott Stump in just a little while this week—I think sometime this week—to talk about how we raise funds for that. But we wanted to do that while it was still on everyone's mind and people forgot about it.

I think the question that I have, and as a scientist, and it makes a difficult when you don't know the etiology of a disease, it's very difficult. You end up treating symptoms. And they may vary. And I found that one of the great things that used to really bother me when I was in practice was, if we didn't know what was wrong with you, we either said it was a virus or you were nervous. I mean, that's basically what you're doing. And I hope we're not doing that here. I don't think so. I think good, honest people looked at the data. I think it's very, very hard to assimilate this.

And the question I have for anybody on the panel, have you looked at the oil workers who put the fires out? Have we looked at the cohorts there in Kuwait? Right now, there are people that still live in Kuwait that were there. Did they have these symptoms? Is there—are there—when we looked at the cohort who were in the service but weren't deployed versus the ones who did—now, I think the Institute of Medicine did that. I think that's the cohort they looked at. You have a built-in group of people right there in Kuwait who were there during the war in Iraq. And has anyone who served in the current conflict in Iraq, now that it's been— we've been out of there for a while, have they had any symptoms? A lot of questions.

Ms. WHITE. Well, to answer some of your questions, the—there have been studies on subgroups of people within the Gulf theatre who had very specific kinds of exposures. So there is a bunch of research out on the pesticide applicators. And we know a lot about what pesticides they were exposed to, how much, what it did to their health. There is a study that's being done at Harvard that I'm participating in on the Kuwaiti population. They do—the people that were there then do have increased symptoms. We're trying to figure out what it means because the surveys that they used and so on didn't exactly address it the way we would address Gulf War illness.

The other point I want to make is that the exposure scenario in the Gulf War theatre was very complex. And comparing deployed to undeployed veterans does not always tell you what happened to people who were in specific places with specific kinds of high exposures. So the standard that we tried to ask for on the Research Advisory Committee (RAC) and in the Cortex paper that I just wrote is looking at people within—who were deployed to the Gulf and who were exposed versus who were not exposed and who were in certain locations.

Mr. ROE. Well, I was going to say, because I know probably the Chairman, when you're in the military, sometimes you don't know where you are. I know that I have been deployed in places I didn't know where I was. And I've—as a matter of fact, I've asked that question. Where are we? I mean, so are you able to pinpoint—that's a great point you made. Can you do a sort of a spotogram where these folks were? Because you're right: being deployed a hundred miles up here might not be the same as being deployed next to a chemical burn.

Ms. WHITE. Yes.

Mr. ROE. No question that's true.

Ms. WHITE. So where that data came from, and I used a lot of this data when I was head of an environmental hazards center that was funded by the VA, was we asked for data on what troops were where. And we got troop level data on locations in the Gulf. And we used that for some of our research. That's how we knew who was in the area of the Khamisiyah detonations and certain other things. So, yes, those data are there. It took a lot of years to get it because it was in paper in a warehouse. But there are data on who was where, at least at the troop level.

Mr. ROE. At least that's where they think they were supposed to be.

Ms. WHITE. Yes, because not every individual was where their unit was supposed to be.

Mr. ROE. You get—when you get shot at, you're not necessarily where you're supposed to be. You move from that place.

So I guess what I'm—the last question—my time's about expired. But, again, I thank all of you because this is one of the most difficult epidemiologic issues I've ever looked at. Because, again, in—like in Ebola, we knew what caused Ebola. In other diseases like that, where there's a single agent, you can—we know what a—how that goes. We know exactly what an epidemic is going to do. We followed them for centuries. We know what they're going to do. This is much more difficult because you haven't identified a single agent or multiple agents. Or maybe there were one agent here and somebody else is over here so—and did the treatment contribute to it? I mean, did giving the soldier something to prevent it do anything? So I admire you for trying this. This is one of the most different epidemiologic studies I've ever seen.

So I yield back.

Dr. CLANCY. The only thing I would say very briefly is, I mean, I think it's a particular challenge for a chronic ongoing kind of condition, which is different than a sort of acute epidemic, the way that you've described.

The other thing that I would say is, I don't think that we should discount the progress we've made. Cancer would be a perfect example, right, where we've learned a lot through brunt empiricism, because we didn't understand underlying etiology, but we tried a whole lot of treatments first and eventually made a lot of progress.

Mr. COFFMAN. Thank you, Dr. Roe.

Sergeant Major Walz.

Mr. WALZ. Thank you, Chairman, and I thank you all for being here. I think I'll dovetail on that, Dr. Clancy. First of all, thank you for the update on the step pain management plan. I think it's important information with the hearing that's going to be next week up in New Hampshire with Ms. Kuster that, back in 2007, this very issue was out there, and I think great strides were made, and I think you have much to add to the conversation because this is not a VA issue of opioid use and pain. It is a societal issue. So I appreciate that update.

And I think, going back to what you said, I do think you're right on that. I think much progress was made on some of these very difficult ones. Dr. Roe clearly laid out the epidemiology and the challenge of this.

My concern is, though, when do we make a decision that we've tried hard enough or that we've reached that point, because I think the frustration lies in this that I think many—something's happening, and again, we have to have the data, but there's something happening. There's enough people reporting it. All of us are hearing this, and I just wonder—you have to make tough decisions about where funding sources go and where those types of things happen. I think there's belief of many of us that this is going to be difficult, but we have a responsibility to keep going on it.

How do you make a decision—"you" being the VA, if you can speak for that—how do you make a decision on how hard you push on a certain area or how much you do in the research?

Dr. CLANCY. So let me just say, having run a research agency for quite a few years at HHS, this is one of the toughest kinds of decisions to make, and it's really an investment question, right, where do you place your bets in terms of getting to rapid answers and the kind of evidence that you want, and there's no biblically correct strategy in terms of rules to guide you.

The one recommendation I—the very top line recommendation, and I want to emphasize that we've not had a chance to go over this Institute of Medicine report. It's still—the ink is still drying, so to speak. It's actually a prepublication version, I think, we're all looking at, and so forth, and are looking forward to going over it with our Research Advisory Committee very, very carefully. But the notion that we would develop a cohesive, coherent plan with the Department of Defense and, frankly, inviting others, like the Harvard study that Dr. White referenced and so forth, to find out— to really push very hard on this question.

There's a huge proportion of people who were deployed for these two operations, and we don't have any answers. We have some promising signals, and that's exciting. I think some additional genomic studies, as a paper that I'm looking at from Dr. White has pointed out, may help us even more, but that's not coming up with an answer for why our almost a third of these soldiers deployed are struggling.

So I think that this is going to be a tough answer to come up with and a tough strategy to come up with, but it's one that we'd be looking forward to giving you full answers on.

The last thing I would say is, the number I gave you is a very, very conservative estimate because it doesn't count our epidemiological studies. It doesn't count the investments we've made in registries, for example, the Gulf War registry, the burn pits registry, and so forth. And so we're investing more than that, but the question is, have we done enough? And I think the answer to that is no.

Mr. WALZ. No, and I appreciate that because I do think you got on it, too, that the broader issue—I think many of us who have followed the issues on Agent Orange, and there's Vietnam veterans sitting in this room that have pushed on this.

Dr. CLANCY. Sure.

Mr. WALZ. They're concerned on the genetic defect issue of how many generations down the line, you know, beyond spina bifida of what's happening to these children, what's happening to the grandchildren, that's going to come to this, the burn pit, the depleted uranium.

So my question is, are we doing enough? I mean, shame on us if we're not learning that every generation has to come back and fight the fights on these things. Is now the time for a center of excellence on toxic wounds? Is this the time to do that? Does that make the difference, where it brings the force of all of these issues under one? Because the thing I worry about is—I don't want to put Parkinson's research on Agent Orange exposure against Gulf War exposure. And I know you may tell me that's the choices we have to make, the hard ones. So I ask you, is the center of excellence the way to go to bring this under one in-house?

Dr. CLANCY. You know, it may be, and we would love to work with you on that, because no matter when we called it—because I agree with you about the X amount here, Y amount there, who's made the most noise recently, to be crass.

Mr. WALZ. Yes. No, I think that's a true statement, though.

Dr. CLANCY. No matter how you cut it, it's going to have to be an entity that coordinates what we're doing with Defense, with what's going on at HHS, and from a variety of other funders, which would be great, actually, because—but I think we can leverage all of that. We've recently been working with CDC's agency for toxic substances and diseases on the Camp Lejeune issue, and actually, that was very, very productive.

Mr. WALZ. And I think our issue, especially with these toxic wound exposures in battle, it differs from cancer in that the private sector is not investing as much in this because there's—

Dr. CLANCY. Right.

Mr. WALZ [continued].—not—it's a limited universe that's going to be treated by this. So, once we treat them, which we need to do, and cure them, there's not a market for the product necessarily.

Dr. CLANCY. Exactly.

Mr. WALZ. That may be crass, too, but that's the reality of the economics. But, no, I thank you all for that, and I think the commitment here is, is that something happened to these folks. It's real—

Dr. CLANCY. Yeah.

Mr. WALZ [continued].—and they deserve an answer and a treatment.

So I yield back.

Mr. COFFMAN. Thank you, Sergeant Major Walz.

Mr. Huelskamp.

Mr. HUELSKAMP. Thank you, Mr. Chairman.

I appreciate the topic of our hearing today. I'm hearing a lot of contradictory claims and concerns and maybe a conclusion. I want to direct a couple of questions to Dr. Hunt, who I don't think has had an opportunity to participate today on the question and answer, but based on the tenor of a relatively recent presentation you gave called, "A Model for Providing Services for Returning Combat Veterans," it's apparent that, and you others in the VA believe Gulf War illness is a mental disorder. Is that correct?

Dr. HUNT. That is not correct. I'm not sure where you got that information.

Mr. HUELSKAMP. Did you not have a presentation entitled "A Model for Providing Services for Returning Gulf War Veterans"?

Dr. HUNT. Presented where?

Mr. HUELSKAMP. I don't have that, the place of presentation.

Dr. HUNT. I don't believe that, and I have never said that, and I don't—no.

Mr. HUELSKAMP. So this wasn't your presentation then?

Dr. HUNT. It could be. I would have to look at it. I'm not sure.

Mr. HUELSKAMP. Okay. Well, I don't know. You never made a presentation on "A Model Providing Services for Returning Gulf War Veterans"?

Dr. HUNT. I give presentations on that often.

Mr. HUELSKAMP. All right.

Dr. HUNT. But I would like to see it because it certainly is a misinterpretation of what I believe and, I suspect, what I said.

Mr. HUELSKAMP. So do you believe also or otherwise that psychiatric drugs are the best treatment for veterans with Gulf War illness?

Dr. HUNT. I believe that medications should be used for conditions they're indicated for, and psychiatric medications are not indicated for Gulf War illness, per se.

Mr. HUELSKAMP. What kind of treatments would you suggest then?

Dr. HUNT. I think the most—25 years ago, what was going on with me was, I was starting to see people coming back in 1992 and 1993, coming back from the war, and the things that they were saying when they came back were not, "I have Gulf syndrome" or "I have a mystery illness." What they were saying was: "I'm not doing very well. I'm having a lot of trouble. I'm having trouble at home; work's not going well. I can't do my PT for Reserves—Guard and Reserves," and so on.

And our response to that was to set up a clinic for returning combat veterans that really was looking at the various ways that the deployment impacted their health: how it impacted their health physically; how it impacted their health psychologically, emotionally, spiritually; how it affected their families. And we came up with a model of integrated care to support Gulf War veterans. It became the Gulf War Veterans' Clinic.

That eventually morphed into what we call in the VA Deployment Health Clinics, or turned into what we call a Post-Deployment Integrated Care Initiative. I have never—the first veterans that came back, I would not have said, "This is in your head," or "I think this is a mental condition." I would have said: "You're having trouble. I don't know exactly what all is going on, but I know you've been off to war. I know you've been exposed to a lot of things. I know you've had some very difficult experiences, and let's see what we can do to get you back on your feet."

I've had an eye on two things. One is the sort of research that Dr. Golomb and Roberta and Lea Steele have been trying to do to figure out what's the cause of this Gulf War illness that's very discrete. Clearly, we have higher rates of these symptoms and this problem in Gulf War veterans than any other cohort I've ever seen.

The research is important. At the same time, we had to have a way of helping people, and so our clinical focus has been: How can we help you get back on your feet? By providing you with integrated—good integrated care that includes symptom management, that includes medications when they're appropriate, that includes—

Mr. HUELSKAMP. Are the psychiatric drugs most effective, you believe, or what have you seen in—

Dr. HUNT [continued]. I think the most effective thing is good health care, is appropriate evaluations and treatments for diagnosable conditions, getting people resources they need through service-connection. This is the first time we've given service-connection—

Mr. HUELSKAMP. Excuse me, sir. That's general. I'm asking you about psychiatric drugs. Are they effective in the treatment or not?

Dr. HUNT. They are effective in the treatment for indicated conditions. If a person—one of the problems we had—and Anthony, I was thinking about this when you were talking as well—if—because of the suicide issue, if we see Gulf War veterans that have unexplained symptoms or Gulf War illness, they may also have concurrent or co-occurring depression, and they are at risk for suicide, and so it's very important that we don't look at this as either/or, and if a person has a mental health condition, that they get appropriate treatment, which—

Mr. HUELSKAMP. My concern is, it seeks like the psychiatric drug approach seems to be where—the simplest choice for the VA to make.

Dr. HUNT. I would not say that.

Mr. HUELSKAMP. And I appreciate—

Dr. HUNT. I would not say that.

Mr. HUELSKAMP [continued].—you disagreeing with that.

The last thing, I want to ask a question of Dr. Cory-Slechta. In your recommendations, you do suggest no further studies should be undertaken on cause-and-effect relationship because you don't have definitive and verifiable individual veteran exposure information. Is that correct? Is that your recommendation?

Ms. CORY-SLECHTA. There were no measures made of internal exposures of veterans, and there were no measures made even of environmental exposure levels. This is basic principles of toxicology and pharmacology.

Mr. HUELSKAMP. So, in your opinion, then—and I understand that. In your opinion, then, all the previous studies that attempted to determine that, are they invalid then?

Ms. CORY-SLECHTA. I don't think you can rely on self-report, because there will be people who were actually exposed who don't even know it.

Mr. HUELSKAMP. This is not about self-reporting. It's whether you have definitive or verifiable individual veteran exposure.

Ms. CORY-SLECHTA. I think it's possible to get those kinds of measures, and that's what I stressed before, that in the future, we need biomonitoring devices and GPS tracking devices so we can in fact get that kind of information and make those associations.

Mr. HUELSKAMP. And I understand that. I'm just trying to figure out whether you thought we had that in the past, and to me, that calls in question a number of these studies, if we don't have that type information.

Lastly, you did request additional studies of sex-specific and race/ethnicity-specific health conditions. If we don't have the individual exposure information, how do we determine—

Ms. CORY-SLECHTA. Well, there may be—we know a lot of diseases and disorders differ in their manifestations by sex or by race/ethnicity.

Mr. HUELSKAMP. If we don't have the exposure information, which is a key variable, how—

Ms. CORY-SLECHTA. It's a different point.

Mr. HUELSKAMP [continued].—do you study that?

Ms. CORY-SLECHTA. It's a different point. The exposure information, what this committee has said is that we'll never be able to understand how those exposures actually related to these health outcomes. We don't have any objective exposure.

Mr. HUELSKAMP. We don't know whether they have exposure or not is your point.

Ms. CORY-SLECHTA. Sorry?

Mr. HUELSKAMP. We don't know whether they have exposure or not. Is that the answer?

Ms. CORY-SLECHTA. We know there were exposures. What we don't have is actual information for individuals that we would look at it in relation to health outcomes.

Mr. HUELSKAMP. I understand. So—

Ms. CORY-SLECHTA. We know there were exposures.

Mr. HUELSKAMP [continued].—So I don't know how you do your second round of studies that you recommended. You say abandon the first round, but the second round, you're talking about race and sex and—

Ms. CORY-SLECHTA. We're just saying for any health outcomes, because oftentimes, for many different diseases and disorders, there are manifestations, and sometimes their mechanisms differ by sex and by race/ethnicity. In order to really understand and/or treat them, you may be doing it very differently. Heart attack is very different in a man than in a woman, for example.

Mr. HUELSKAMP. Yeah.

Ms. CORY-SLECHTA. So we need to break those out and look at them.

Mr. HUELSKAMP. Thank you, Mr. Chairman. I just found it concerning that the basic exposure information is—we're hearing that, well, we don't know what it is, and so if you take that variable out, I mean, that strikes out a lot of information, a lot of data, and a lot of research would be thrown out by the Institute of Medicine, and we spent a lot of time, attention, and money trying to figure this out, so very concerning.

I yield back.

Mr. COFFMAN. Thank you, Mr. Huelskamp.

We'll have one more round if anybody else has questions. I do have two questions.

Mr. Winnett, could you join us at the table?

Mr. WINNETT. Sure. Can I get a bottle of water first? I just took a Vicodin. Hard to take those on a dry mouth.

Mr. COFFMAN. Mr. Winnett, on your Facebook group related to Gulf War illness, you asked: How many veterans are being referred for psychiatric or psychological treatment?

What kind of response are you getting?

Mr. WINNETT. In a word, overwhelming, sir. Can you hear me okay?

Mr. COFFMAN. Is that on, microphone on?

Mr. WINNETT. In a word, the answer to that question, Congressman, is overwhelming. I might add that, yesterday, we hit the milestone of 10,000 veterans. This is a closed group, and I approve every member and have so for over the last 7 years. Overwhelming. And my written statement for the record includes quite a number of them, but obviously not all of them, but it took some of those that were very compelling, and I think they are self-explanatory if you read my statement as to what the prevailing attitude is about VA's treatment of Gulf War illness.

Mr. COFFMAN. Thank you.

Now, Mr. Binns, could you please come to the table? Mr. Binns, given VA's use of IOM reports in the manner we have discussed, are you aware of any requirements for such reports?

Mr. BINNS. Yes, I am. The Congress ordered these IOM reports, and in the law, it specified very clearly what it wanted the IOM reports to consider. It listed 33 toxic exposures, including all the ones that have been mentioned here, and it asked whether in the medical literature, there was an association between any of those toxic exposures and illness in humans or in animals.

Congress did not ask whether there was data on the individual exposure levels that troops received because it was known, at the time the law was passed, that that information was not available, but it did want to have the information on animals, because most studies of toxic substances are done in animals.

When VA contracted for these studies, however, they did not contract for considering animal studies. And the Institute of Medicine was a willing accomplice in that it removed consideration of animal studies from its standards of evidence, which it had used in the case of Agent Orange evaluations for Vietnam veterans. So the action taken was exactly the opposite of what Congress ordered, and as a result, that entire stack of reports, which you see, no IOM report has ever considered animal studies in its conclusions, and no IOM report has ever found an association between a toxic exposure and the illnesses that we're talking about today.

And I want to just clarify, because there has been a lot of discussion today about how complex this is. And, certainly, going forward, it is complex to find treatments, but well worthwhile. But what is not complex is understanding why these veterans are ill. You do not have to measure each veteran and have a monitor on them to know that.

Our report, the report of the Research Advisory Committee that was done in 2008—here it is—it researches very firm conclusions on the fact that these illnesses were caused by toxic exposures, notably the ones Dr. White mentioned, PB and pesticides. There is no dispute about that if you consider animal research. But the IOM has never considered the animal research. They talk about it, they have paragraphs on it, but when you reach the conclusions, they use a standard of evidence which excludes animal studies.

Please read my submission, and you will see that in detail that the entire IOM reports—if you read the reports, they're very clear. They're very honest. They say: We don't consider these animal studies. And we're talking about basic things here. Here's 2 pages with 23 studies of the effect of low level sarin, such as was experienced in Kamasia that was considered by the Research Advisory Committee and has never been considered by the IOM.

Dr. Cory-Slechta's report on page 139 says that she didn't consider the animal studies because they were relying on earlier IOM reports. Well, if you read the earlier IOM reports, as I indicated in my written submission, they didn't consider them either. These are the basic studies that say the toxic substances are toxic.

So the whole IOM series of Gulf War and health reports is a stack of cards, and the same dishonest standard is being applied to current veterans of Iraq and Afghanistan who have been exposed to burn pits. Once again, there is no consideration of the standard that Congress itself established.

Mr. COFFMAN. Thank you, Mr. Binns.

Ranking Member Kuster, you are now recognized for 5 minutes.

Ms. KUSTER. Yeah. Thank you.

This is a question for Dr. Clancy. And, again, my exposure and my experience doesn't compare to anyone serving in wartime, but part of the complication that I experienced with my lungs was, I was told that I had the lungs of a 90-year-old smoker. And I've never smoked a day in my life, and I consider myself a healthy person, but that's the kind of damage that can be done.

I'm much better now. But I'm curious—and this goes to Dr. Clancy, maybe Dr. Hunt—on the long-term impacts—well, we know from the IOM and just generally that cancers have a long latency period, 20 to 30 years in the case of lung cancer. This is a quote from the Lung Cancer Alliance, from the written statement: The median age for cancer diagnosis in the United States is 65, 70 for lung cancer, and the median age of Gulf War veterans, 1991, was 28. So, add 25 years, we're coming up on this cohort of veterans being 50 years or older, and I'm wondering, is there any action being undertaken by the VA—or could we encourage you to do that—where we would be providing lung cancer screening to Gulf War veterans that we have on the registry, or at least an initiative VA-wide, where we would put the word out for Gulf cancer veterans to get this type of screening? Can you tell me the status and just what that would look like and how we can move forward?

Dr. CLANCY. So, just to be clear, we have pretty well developed cancer registries for most of the major cancers, and I think the Institute of Medicine report was very clear that that would probably be the most fruitful place to identify an increased incidence.

We could certainly explore lung cancer screening for some of these folks, and I actually think that's a very intriguing idea. About 60,000 people have voluntarily signed up to enroll in the burn pits registry. The only caveat—but again, I think this will be interesting to learn. The lung cancer screening studies were done on smokers. Whether it will be as productive in identifying early nodules and so forth in people who have lung damage for another reason is an open question.

Ms. KUSTER. Yeah.

Dr. CLANCY. I will say it's something the VA has been looking at for a few years, not just can we get veteran screening, but also can we do the appropriate follow-up, because the price tag on reducing mortality rate for lung cancer is the only thing we've got, right, is this new kind of screening; it reduces mortality by 20 percent. Nothing else we've ever done works like that.

Ms. KUSTER. Yeah.

Dr. CLANCY. The flip side of it, though, is you have a lot of false positives, so people need to be followed up very, very carefully, and we've been looking into that for several years.

Dr. HUNT. The other important thing for the Committee to know is that our approaches to more proactively addressing exposure concerns following deployment are sort of demonstrated very clearly through the airborne hazard and open burn pit registry. Now, when folks come back from Iraq and Afghanistan, they can go online; they can document their symptoms, their concerns, their exposures. It goes into the clinical record. They come in, and they have an exam, so we're really starting the moment people come back to look at potential sequelae.

Ms. KUSTER. So maybe what we're talking about then would be to take that approach and go back to the Gulf War veterans to bring them in to that. And I understand we don't have the specificity. I get the frustration—

Dr. CLANCY. Yeah.

Ms. KUSTER [continued].—from the science side of wanting to know, but I also feel that people have had exposure, and without even knowing the specificity, at least we would have an understanding. A 20 percent drop in mortality is significant, so—and I just want to associate myself with the remarks of Mr. Walz that maybe that is the approach that we need, is a center of excellence for toxic exposure, toxic wounds. And I also think that, once again, the VA could be on the cutting edge for the civilian population in terms of understanding our exposure to all kinds of toxic substances.

Dr. HUNT. And that's why engaging people in care is so important, too, because the best way to pick up malignancies is to have people involved in regular care so—

Ms. KUSTER. Right.

Dr. HUNT [continued].—So prescribed screening occurs, and so we—if people have symptoms, we're more likely to pick up—pick things up more quickly.

Ms. KUSTER. Right. And I think that, this way, you can bring people back in and, through their regular care, have the conversation about, we would recommend—and I understand, look, CTs for everybody in the world is going to be expensive, but to me, it's very important that we show that kind of care and concern.

I wasn't in Congress 25 years ago. I regret that people were treated this way, and I think we have a bipartisan support here to do better going forward. And, again, thank you for your service and, for all of you, for your interest today.

Mr. COFFMAN. Thank you, Ranking Member Kuster.

Our thanks to the witnesses. You are now excused.

Today, we have had a chance to hear about the problems that exist within the Department of Veterans Affairs with regard to treatment of and current health outcomes for veterans suffering from Gulf War illness. The lack of progress that has been made by the Department in the 3 years that have passed since many of these problems were highlighted by this Subcommittee is both frustrating and disconcerting.

I believe Gulf War veterans deserve better, so I will be exploring options on how to best address these matters in the coming weeks.

I ask unanimous consent that all Members have 5 legislative days to revise and extend their remarks and include extraneous material.

Without objection, so ordered.

I would like to, once again, thank all of our witnesses and audience members for joining in today's conversation.

With that, this hearing is adjourned.

[Whereupon, at 5:58 p.m., the Subcommittee was adjourned.]

APPENDIX

Prepared Statement of Deborah Cory-Slechta, Ph.D.

Good morning, Chairman Miller, Ranking Member Kuster, and members of the Committee. My name is Deborah Cory-Slechta. I am a Professor of Environmental Medicine, Pediatrics and Public Health Sciences, and Acting Chair of the Department of Environmental Medicine at the University of Rochester School of Medicine. I served as the Chair of the Committee on Gulf War and Health, Volume 10: Update of Health Effects of Serving in the Gulf War of the National Academies of Sciences, Engineering, and Medicine. The National Academy of Sciences was chartered by Congress in 1863 to advise the government on matters of science and technology and later expanded to include the National Academies of Engineering and Medicine.

The Institute of Medicine (IOM), part of the National Academies of Sciences, Engineering, and Medicine, released its 10th report on Gulf War and Health on February 11 of this year. The committee that I chaired was asked to review and evaluate the scientific and medical literature regarding associations between illness and exposure to toxic agents, environmental or wartime hazards, or preventive medicines or vaccines associated with Gulf War service and to pay particular attention to neurological disorders (e.g., Parkinson's disease, multiple sclerosis, amyotrophic lateral sclerosis, and migraines), cancer (especially brain cancer and lung cancer), and chronic multisymptom illness (also known as Gulf War illness). Volume 10 updated two earlier Gulf War and Health reports, Volume 4, published in 2006, and Volume 8 published in 2010. The committee made recommendations for future research on Gulf War veterans. I should note that the committee was composed of experts in neurology, epidemiology, pain, psychiatry, neurocognitive disorders, environmental health and toxicology; and clinicians and researchers, none of whom received funding from Gulf War illness research programs.

For the most part, the Volume 10 committee followed the approach used by earlier committees. It held two public sessions at which it heard from representatives of VA, several Gulf War veterans and veteran service organizations, Gulf War researchers, and representatives of the VA Research Advisory Committee on Gulf War Veterans' Illnesses. The committee did not address policy issues, such as service connection, compensation, or the cause of or treatment for Gulf War illness. The committee conducted an extensive literature search and reviewed the Volumes 4 and 8 primary and secondary epidemiologic studies and the conclusions reached by those committees. Other types of studies-such as animal toxicology, neuroimaging, and genetics-were also considered.

Primary studies had to be published in a peer-reviewed journal or other rigorously peer-reviewed publication; demonstrate rigorous methods (for example, have an appropriate control group and include adjustments for confounders); include information on a persistent (not acute) health outcome; use appropriate laboratory testing, if applicable; and have a study population that was generalizable to and representative of the Gulf War veteran population. Secondary studies were those studies that did not necessarily meet all the criteria of a primary study. Many of the secondary studies relied on self-reports of various diagnoses rather than an examination by a health professional or a medical record review.

The committee used the same categories of association relating health conditions to Gufl War deployment as used by previous Gulf War and Health and other IOM committees that have evaluated scientific literature, that is:

- Sufficient Evidence of a Causal Relationship
- Sufficient Evidence of an Association
- Limited/Suggestive Evidence of an Association
- Inadequate/Insufficient Evidence to Determine Whether an Association Exists
- Limited/Suggestive Evidence of No Association

The committee found that in spite of the many millions of dollars that have been spent on researching the health of Gulf War veterans there has been little substantial progress in our understanding of their health, particularly of Gulf War illness. The Volume 10 committee found little evidence to warrant changes to the Volume 8 conclusions regarding the strength of the association between deployment to the Gulf War and adverse health outcomes. Veterans who were deployed to the Gulf War do not appear to have an increased risk for many long-term health conditions with the exceptions of PTSD, Gulf War illness, chronic fatigue syndrome, functional gastrointestinal conditions, generalized anxiety disorder, depression, and substance abuse. The committee's conclusions are briefly summarized in the Box 1.

BOX 1

Summary of Conclusions Regarding Associations Between Deployment

to the Gulf War and Specific Health Conditions

Sufficient Evidence of a Causal Relationship

- Posttraumatic stress disorder (PTSD)

Sufficient Evidence of an Association

- Generalized anxiety disorder, depression, and substance abuse (particularly alcohol abuse)
- Gastrointestinal symptoms consistent with functional gastrointestinal disorders such as irritable bowel syndrome and functional dyspepsia
- Chronic fatigue syndrome
- Gulf War illness

Limited/Suggestive Evidence of an Association

- Amyotrophic lateral sclerosis (ALS)
- Fibromyalgia and chronic widespread pain
- Self-reported sexual difficulties

Inadequate/Insufficient Evidence to Determine Whether an Association Exists

- Any cancer
- Cardiovascular conditions or conditions of the blood and blood-forming organs
- Endocrine, nutritional, and metabolic conditions
- Neurodegenerative diseases other than ALS
- Neurocognitive and neurobehavioral performance
- Migraines and other headache disorders
- Other neurologic conditions
- Respiratory conditions
- Structural gastrointestinal conditions
- Skin conditions
- Musculoskeletal system conditions
- Genitourinary conditions
- Specific birth defects
- Adverse pregnancy outcomes (e.g., miscarriage, stillbirth, preterm birth, and low birth weight)
- Fertility problems
- Increased mortality from any cancer, any neurologic disease (including multiple sclerosis, Alzheimer's disease, Parkinson's disease, and ALS), respiratory disease, or gastrointestinal disease

Limited/Suggestive Evidence of No Association

- Objective measures of peripheral neurologic conditions
- Multiple sclerosis
- Mortality from cardiovascular, infectious, or parasitic diseases
- Decreased lung function
- Mortality due to mechanical trauma or other external causes

As requested in its statement of task, the committee had additional discussions pertaining to Gulf War illness, neurologic conditions, and lung and brain cancer on those health conditions and other aspects of Gulf War veteran health.

Gulf War Illness. Gulf War illness is the signature adverse health outcome of having served in the Persian Gulf region. Multiple studies found that some Gulf War veterans, regardless of their country of origin and their different deployment-related exposures, have persistent, debilitating, and varying symptoms (such as joint and muscle pain, fatigue, and cognitive problems) of Gulf War illness. In spite of over 2 decades of research to define, diagnose, and treat Gulf War illness, little progress has been made in elucidating the pathophysiologic mechanisms that underlie it, the exposures that may have caused it, or treatments that are generally effective for it.

Gulf War illness is not an easily defined or diagnosed condition. The committee concluded that it is not a psychosomatic illness, but it does present with diverse symptoms, many of which overlap with other health conditions such as chronic fatigue syndrome, neurodegenerative disorders, and musculoskeletal problems. Based on available research data, it does not appear that a single mechanism can explain the multitude of symptoms seen in Gulf War illness, and the committee found it unlikely that a single definitive causal agent would be identified this many years after the war. Furthermore, most Gulf War illness studies have excluded the psychological aspects of the condition with regard to both diagnosis and treatment although veterans report symptoms such as chronic pain and sleep disturbances that may be amenable to psychological therapies, alone or in conjunction with other treatments.

The committee concluded that although the existence of an animal model would be advantageous for identifying and evaluating treatment strategies for Gulf War illness, it cautions that developing such an animal model is precluded by the absence of any objective measures of chemical and nonchemical exposures during Gulf War service, let alone the frequency, duration, or dose of those exposures, or the highly likely interactive effects of multiple exposures.

Neurologic Conditions. The committee found little new information pertaining to multiple sclerosis, Parkinson's disease, Alzheimer's disease, or migraines. ALS is the only neurologic disease for which the committee found limited/suggestive evidence for an association with deployment to the Gulf War. The committee concluded that further follow-up of this uniformly fatal disease is warranted. The Gulf War veteran population is still young with respect to the development of other neurodegenerative diseases; therefore, the effects of deployment on their incidence and prevalence may not yet be obvious.

Lung Cancer and Brain Cancer. The committee found the evidence for brain cancer to be inadequate/insufficient and it found no statistically significant increase in the current risk of brain cancer in deployed Gulf War veterans compared with their nondeployed counterparts. This finding is mirrored in another recent IOM study. With regard to lung cancer, the committee notes that the 10–15 years of follow-up that have been reported may not have been adequate to account for the long latency of this disease. Although one new study found an increased incidence of lung cancer for deployed versus nondeployed veterans, neither veteran group had a greater risk when compared with the general population, and the study did not indicate smoking status. Thus, the committee found that the evidence continues to be inadequate/insufficient to determine whether deployed Gulf War veterans are at increased risk of having any cancer, including lung and brain cancer. The relative rarity of cancers such as brain cancer argues for larger studies with adequate power to detect them.

Other Health Outcomes. The committee finds that sufficient time has elapsed to determine that Gulf War deployed veterans do not have an increased incidence of circulatory, hematologic, respiratory, musculoskeletal, structural gastrointestinal, genitourinary, reproductive, or chronic skin conditions compared with their nondeployed counterparts. As Gulf War veterans age, it will be more difficult to differentiate the effects of deployment from the natural effects of aging on morbidity and mortality. Furthermore, the association of deployment to the Gulf War with PTSD, anxiety disorders, substance abuse, and depression is well established, and further studies to assess whether there is an association are not warranted.

Although there are well-known differences in disease profiles according to sex and race/ethnicity, few studies on Gulf War veterans specifically report outcomes for women or minorities, although many veteran studies adjust for sex and race/ethnicity in their analyses. This lack of distinction is important and makes it imperative that researchers report sex-specific and race/ethnicity-specific outcomes, particularly in large cohorts and where population subgroups may be oversampled.

In conclusion, what is striking about this and prior Gulf War and Health committees' findings is that the health conditions found to be associated with Gulf War deployment are primarily functional medical disorders such as Gulf War illness and irritable bowel syndrome, and mental health disorders such as PTSD and depression. What links these conditions is that they have no objective medical diagnostic tests and are diagnosed based on subjective symptom reporting.

To be clear, the committee recognizes that Gulf War illness is a distinct medical condition with symptoms that affect many organs and organ systems including the brain; these symptoms include cognitive difficulties, memory problems, and headaches. Many other chronic illnesses from kidney disease to cancer also can affect the brain.

Based on its conclusions regarding the association between deployment to the Gulf War and the health conditions seen in Gulf War veterans 25 years after the war, the committee made the following recommendations:

- **Recognize the connections and complex relationships between brain and physical functioning and should not exclude any aspect of Gulf War illness with respect to improving its diagnosis and treatment.**
- **The Department of Veterans Affairs and the Department of Defense should develop a joint and cohesive strategy on incorporating emerging diagnostic technologies and personalized approaches to medical care into sufficiently powered future research to inform studies of Gulf War illness and related health conditions.**
- **The Department of Veterans Affairs should continue to conduct follow-up assessments of Gulf War veterans for neurodegenerative diseases that have long latencies and are associated with aging; these include amyotrophic lateral sclerosis, Alzheimer's disease, and Parkinson's disease.**
- **The Department of Veterans Affairs should conduct further assessments of cancer incidence, prevalence, and mortality because of the long latency of some cancers. Such studies should maximize the use of cancer registries and other relevant sources, data, and approaches, and should have sufficient sample sizes to account for relatively rare cancers and to be able to report sex-specific and race/ethnicity-specific information.**
- **Further studies to assess the incidence and prevalence of circulatory, hematologic, respiratory, musculoskeletal, structural gastrointestinal, genitourinary, reproductive, endocrine and metabolic, chronic skin, and mental health conditions due to deployment in the Gulf War should not be undertaken. Rather, future research related to these conditions should focus on ensuring that Gulf War veterans with them receive timely and effective treatment.**
- **Without definitive and verifiable individual veteran exposure information, further studies to determine cause-and-effect relationships between Gulf War chemical exposures and health conditions in Gulf War veterans should not be undertaken.**
- **Sex-specific and race/ethnicity-specific health conditions should be determined and reported in future studies of Gulf War veterans. In addition, selected prior studies (e.g., large cohort studies) should be reviewed to determine whether reanalysis of the data to assess for possible sex-specific and race/ethnic-specific health conditions is feasible.**
- **Future Gulf War research should place top priority on the identification and development of effective therapeutic interventions and management strategies for Gulf War illness. The Department of Veterans Affairs should support research to determine how such treatments can be widely disseminated and implemented in all health care settings.**

The committee believes that it is time that research efforts move forward and focus on improving treatment and medical management of veterans for Gulf War illness, including all affected organs and systems of the body. Further exploration of treatments and management strategies for the symptoms of Gulf War illness, even in the absence of a definitive etiology, is warranted.

Finally, the committee wants to emphasize that it did not recommend that research on the health of Gulf War veterans be stopped. Rather, the committee found that research that continues to seek a causal link between Gulf War illness or other health conditions found in Gulf War veterans and specific chemical exposures, such as PB, sarin, or pesticides, is not likely to yield useful information. Many millions of dollars have been spent on this research with few tangible results and those resources are more likely to have an impact if focused on treatment and management strategies for these veterans.

Thank you and I am pleased to answer any questions that you may have.

☞

Prepared Statement of Roberta F. White, Ph.D

Gulf War illness and the health of Gulf War veterans: 25 years of progress and set-backs

It is the 25th anniversary of the Gulf War. Our veterans won this conflict in less than a week. However, concern remains high that the troops who produced this victory are and will remain ill, without legitimate acknowledgement of their health problems and the associated disabilities, and without effective treatment options now or in the future.

Despite decades of scientific evidence to the contrary, the VA and the Institute of Medicine have recently produced documents that minimize the poor health of these veterans by terming their illnesses as "functional " disorders, a medical term for psychiatric illness. This injustice is then compounded by a treatment guideline that suggests ineffective, unproven, purely palliative, and potentially harmful treatments for Gulf War illness that focus on psychiatric symptomatology.

I speak as a clinician/scientist who has worked with Gulf War veterans clinically and in research for over 20 years. My work on Gulf War illness is part of an overall clinical and research career in which I have studied the effects of exposures to neurotoxic chemicals on adults and children. For eight years, until last fall, I served as scientific director of the Research Advisory Committee on Gulf War Veterans Illnesses.

Science of Gulf War illness

It has been known since a year or two after their return from the Gulf that a subset of Gulf War veterans was experiencing debilitating physical illness. (In fact, the Department of Public Health at VA engaged clinical and research personnel at the Boston VA Medical Center, including myself, in trying to figure out what was going on with the veterans).

Research beginning at that time and continuing to the present has produced a consensus of scientific knowledge about this illness.

- Dozens of studies in multiple countries reveal that approximately 30% of the 1991 Gulf War veteran population suffers from a characteristic pattern of physical health symptoms. This research has further revealed that this pattern of health problems was seen in Gulf War veterans, but not veterans of other conflicts (such as Bosnia), and that veteran populations from multiple coalition forces from the Gulf War experienced the same disorder.

The health problems of Gulf War veterans are not vague and extremely variable, as is often suggested. There are two case definitions of the illness-the Kansas definition and the Centers for Disease Control definition-that clearly allow researchers and clinicians to decide whether an individual Gulf War veteran has the illness. These definitions were supported by the Institute of Medicine in its Volume 9 report for use in clinical and research work. I cannot think of any illness in which all patients have exactly the same symptoms-diagnosis of diseases and disorders is based on critical masses of signs and symptoms that cluster together to fit a case definition. Gulf War illness is not different from any other disorder in this way.

- This illness is not the result of stress or other psychiatric factors. It has been known since the 1990s that post-traumatic stress disorder occurs at far lower rates in Gulf War populations than Gulf War illness. Rates are typically less than 10%, in contrast to the 30% for Gulf War illness. Furthermore, research conducted in veterans with Gulf War illness has repeatedly shown that post-traumatic stress disorder and other psychiatric disorders do not predict whether a veteran will have Gulf War illness, that is rates of Gulf War illness are not significantly higher in Gulf War veterans with psychiatric diagnoses.
- Research over the past 20 years has also shown that occurrence of Gulf War illness is associated with exposures to chemicals present in the Gulf War theater, especially pesticides and use of pyridostigmine bromide (and possibly other chemicals, including nerve gas agent sarin and particulate matter from oil well fires).

Epidemiologic, clinical, and animal research involving Gulf War veterans and other populations with similar types of exposures has converged to show that these chemicals affect the central nervous and immune systems, producing chronic signs and symptoms that affect multiple body systems.

As suggested by the Institute of Medicine in its recent Volume 10 report, there is a mind/body continuum here. However, it is not that these veterans have a psychiatric condition that is affecting their physical health; it is that exposures to the chemicals present in the Gulf theater affect brain systems that mediate cognition, emotion, and immune function simultaneously. Thus, ill veterans have multiple cognitive, physical and emotional complaints and signs and symptoms.

The previous Institute of Medicine report, Volume 8, reflected the scientific consensus on Gulf War illness that I have just described, concluding that "[t]he excess of unexplained medical symptoms reported by deployed Gulf war veterans cannot be reliably ascribed to any known psychiatric disorder" and that "it is likely that Gulf War illness results from an interplay of genetic and environmental factors."

Like the reports of the Research Advisory Committee, the Volume 8 Institute of Medicine report called for rigorous research to find effective treatments for the illness, including "studies to identify . . . modifications of DNA structure related to environmental exposures, . . . signatures of immune activation, or brain changes identified by sensitive imaging measures."

Effective treatments for Gulf War illness and other illnesses induced by exposures that damage the brain do not exist. This is true for exposures such as lead, mercury and solvents as well as the pesticides, pyridostigmine bromide, low-level chemical warfare agents, and air pollutants to which our Gulf War veterans were exposed. However, recent research has identified potential treatments of Gulf War illness that target specific nervous system and immunological mechanisms. These treatments are now being piloted. They are consistent with the types of treatments recommended in the Volume 8 Institute of Medicine report and hold promise for effective treatment of Gulf War veterans, other veterans who experience chemical exposures, future troops at risk of similar exposures, and people who are exposed to pesticides occupationally and environmentally.

The progress made over the past 20 years in understanding the mechanisms and causes of Gulf War illness, the physiological effects of exposure to chemicals such as pesticides, and the treatment of these effects is extremely exciting for the health of the military and the population as a whole. The scientific findings from this research hold great scientific promise. In addition, they are the only source of hope for veterans with Gulf War illness who are suffering from the disorder and wish to lead healthier, more productive lives.

VA treatment recommendations

However, recent recommendations from VA concerning the diagnosis and treatment of ill Gulf War veterans threaten the viability of the promise emanating from two decades of research. These recommendations are summarized in a document entitled, VA/DoD Clinical Practice Guideline: Management of Chronic Multi-symptom Illness, 2014.

The recommendations contained in this document are regressive in terms of the knowledge that science and medicine have provided on the disorder. They are consistent with the stance that VA has taken since the Gulf War illness issue was first discovered in the early 1990s, when VA staff published papers saying that the health problems of Gulf War veterans represented post-traumatic stress disorder or "effects seen in all wars," statements that were made before any scientific data had been collected on ill Gulf War veterans.

The treatment recommendations include immediate referral for mental health evaluation. In addition, cognitive behavioral therapy is suggested. This is a palliative treatment that might allow veterans to manage their lives better but was already found in a major VA study to help less than 6% of GW veteran patients and to provide only a 1 point improvement on a scale of 100.

Even worse, when these palliative therapies do not satisfy the patient, the treatment guidelines recommend eleven drugs, ten of them psychiatric. All eleven drugs are noted in the guidelines to have significant adverse side effects, including suicidal ideation. Even more disturbing, these medications have not been studied with regard to effectiveness in the treatment of Gulf War illness. They are not the medications or treatment approaches of choice among the VA clinicians with extensive clinical treatment experience who have discussed their approaches with the Research Advisory Committee on Gulf War Veterans Illnesses. And the advice of such experts does not seem to have been solicited for this treatment document.

In my experience as a neuropsychologist, I have had many patients whose neurological illnesses were initially thought to be psychiatric-the term "functional" was, in fact, sometimes used to describe them. These patients include people with multiple sclerosis, small vessel strokes, dementias and exposures to chemicals such as solvents or mercury. Treating Gulf War illness with an antidepressant is akin to treating multiple sclerosis with one. The patient might feel a little more optimistic, but the medication will do nothing to reverse or prevent the brain damage that the multiple sclerosis disease process is inflicting on his or her brain.

Furthermore, the VA treatment document says its advice is also appropriate for mild traumatic brain injury, suggesting that recent Iraq and Afghanistan veterans who suffered blast injuries from improvised explosive device (IED) exposures should also be treated as psychiatric cases.

IOM report Volume 10

The recent Volume 10 Institute of Medicine report further contributes to the worsening plights of ill Gulf War veterans by minimizing their health problems and again placing a psychiatric cast on them.

This report was written by a committee that (purposefully) included no one with clinical experience treating Gulf War veterans or in-depth epidemiological expertise in the phenomenology of Gulf War illness.

The report supports the VA stance that Gulf War illness is a functional disorder without evaluating the extensive scientific evidence that demonstrates just the opposite.

Although the Volume 10 Institute of Medicine report states that the science has not changed since the Volume 8 report, its conclusions fly in the face of the scientific consensus on Gulf War illness that I have described, a consensus that was embraced in the Volume 8 report. The Volume 10 report distorts and disavows the Volume 8 report's finding that Gulf War illness "cannot be reliably ascribed to any known psychiatric disorder" by saying that the illness "cannot be fully explained by any .psychiatric disorder."

Unlike prior reports that support mechanistic scientific research on Gulf War illness, Volume 10 suggests that "it is time research efforts focus on the [mind-body] interconnectedness" and that "further research to determine the relationships between Gulf War exposures and health conditions in Gulf War veterans should not be undertaken."

To recommend stopping research into the mechanisms underlying the disease, just as research into these mechanisms has begun to make real progress, is shockingly short-sighted. And to suggest that psychiatric research has been neglected could not be further from the truth.

During the fifteen years after the war, federal Gulf War research focused mainly on psychiatric issues. For example, 51% of VA research funding in 2003 for Gulf War illness focused on psychological stress and psychiatric illness. This research revealed that the answer to the Gulf War illness problem could not be found in the psychiatric arena. It is unthinkable that the scientific progress now being made should be halted and to return to that era.

Conclusion

When I think of the problem of Gulf War illness and the health problems and disabilities of the many Gulf War veterans whom I know or have evaluated, I am painfully reminded of the veterans of World War I who were exposed to mustard gas in the trenches of Europe. The gas was known to be present and widespread and it was known that mustard was designed to make people very sick or kill them. However, these veterans did not receive support for their health problems or the hardships their families endured due to their disabilities when they returned from combat.

We are experiencing the same phenomenon with the 1991 Gulf War. It is well known and established that Gulf War veterans were exposed to poisons such as pesticides, pyridostigmine bromide, sarin gas and air pollutants from oil well fires that are harmful to health. However, groups like the Institute of Medicine and VA state that with current technology we cannot identify exactly which chemicals and which dosages each individual veteran was exposed to. This leads them to claim that we do not know enough to conclude that the Gulf War veteran population was overexposed to toxic chemicals and that individual veterans are ill. This is not the approach to population environmental health problems that we should expect.

Prepared Statement of Anthony Hardie

Thank you, Chairman Coffman, Ranking Member Kuster, and Members of the Committee for today's hearing and for this opportunity to appear before you.

I'm Anthony Hardie, a 1991 Gulf War and Somalia veteran, and Director of Veterans for Common Sense. I've provided testimony on several previous occasions, but today is especially notable.

Twenty-five years ago tonight, we launched the ground war of Operation Desert Storm and successfully liberated Kuwait. Tonight, I would like us to remember and honor of the nearly 300 of our fellow Gulf War men and women who made the ultimate sacrifice. I would also like us to remember and honor the nearly 700,000 veterans of the Persian Gulf War, who under the direction of our military leaders led our broad international Coalition to decisive military victory.

"Our" war was relatively short: just a five-month buildup, and then a six-week war before a swift military victory. However, you've heard my personal experiences before, and you've heard the stories of many other Gulf War veterans, and as this Committee knows, between one-fourth and one-third of us returned home with serious and debilitating health issues now known as Gulf War Illness. And, we faced a new battle, a much longer war · a war to obtain effective healthcare and VA assistance from entrenched government officials who seemed intent on proving there was nothing wrong with so many Gulf War veterans, that it was all in our heads, just stress, the same as after every war.

1998 PERSIAN GULF WAR VETERANS LEGISLATION

It took almost eight years after the war before our major legislative victory, with the enactment of the Persian Gulf War Veterans Act of 1998 (Title XVI, PL 105–277) and the Veterans Programs Enhancement Act of 1998 (PL 105–368, Title I-"Provisions Relating to Veterans of Persian Gulf War and Future Conflicts") · two landmark bills that set the framework for Gulf War veterans' healthcare, research, and disability benefits.

For those of us involved in fighting for the creation and enactment of these laws, they seemed clear and straightforward, with a comprehensive, statutorily-mandated plan that would guarantee research, treatments, appropriate benefits, and help ensure that lessons learned from our experiences would result in never again allowing what happened to us to happen to future generations of warriors.

The legislation included a long list of known Gulf War exposures. VA was to presume our exposure to all of these, and then, with the assistance of the National Academy of Sciences (NAS), evaluate each exposure for associated adverse health outcomes in humans and animals. In turn, the VA Secretary would consider the reports by the NAS's Institute of Medicine (IOM), "and all other sound medical and scientific information and analyses available," and make determinations granting presumptive conditions. There was a new guarantee of VA health care. There would also be a new national center for the study of war-related illnesses and post-deployment health issues, which would conduct and promote research regarding their etiologies, diagnosis, treatment, and prevention and promote the development of appropriate health policies, including monitoring, medical recordkeeping, risk communication, and use of new technologies. There was to be an effective methodology for treatment development and evaluation, a medical education curriculum, and outreach to Gulf War veterans. Research findings were to be thoroughly publicized. To ensure the federal government's proposed research studies, plans, and strategies stayed focused and on track, VA was to appoint a research advisory committee that included Gulf War veterans · presumably those who were ill and affected · and their representatives.

Instead, we learned that enactment of those laws was just another battle in our long war.

From the beginning, VA officials fought against implementing these laws, dragging their feet and upending their implementation.

The creation of the "national center" never met Gulf War veterans' expectations. The long list of toxic exposures never led to a single exposure-related presumption. Many of the exposures were never even considered, and those that were didn't include evaluation of the health effects in laboratory animals with respect to likely health outcomes in ill Gulf War veterans. The research never led to effective, evidence-based treatments and indeed had little treatment focus until after Congress established a treatment-focused research program outside of VA.

And only after significant pressure and a change in Administrations did VA finally establish the research advisory committee (RAC) · more than three years after the statutorily mandated January 1, 1999 deadline. But, VA then systematically ignored its recommendations, and diminished its findings. When it sharpened its criticism of VA's failures related to Gulf War veterans, VA staff led measures to substantially diminish its charter and discharge all of its members.

As a last ditch effort to call attention to VA's myriad failures of Gulf War veterans, I led Gulf War veterans' resignations from the RAC in June 2013. Subsequently, the House unanimously passed legislation that would have restored and enhanced the research advisory committee and helped Gulf War veterans, for which we remain grateful. Unfortunately, the Senate failed to take action and the bill died in Congress.

I served on the RAC for eight years and remain deeply impressed by the broad knowledge, demonstrated commitment, and impressive accomplishments aimed at solving Gulf War Illness of the scientists and doctors who served on and appeared before the panel. And, I remain proud of the work of dozens of researchers and Gulf War veteran stakeholders who came together to produce a comprehensive strategic plan aimed at solving Gulf War Illness, identifying other health conditions in Gulf War veterans, and helping achieve the laudable goals of the 1998 Gulf War legislation. Sadly for ill Gulf War veterans, nearly all of the provisions of that research strategic plan remain unimplemented, like so much of the rest of VA's half steps in implementing and achieving the goals of the 1998 legislation.

And in a 2013 hearing by this Committee, we learned from a top VA epidemiologist-turned-whistleblower many of the sordid details of officials within the VA's Office of Public Health who failed to ask the right questions in research that would lead to showing the real post-deployment health outcomes for Gulf War and other veterans, and often obfuscated research findings when they showed results that might show significant health outcomes.

That leads us to today.

NEW IOM REPORT

Two weeks ago, the NAS's Institute of Medicine (IOM) released its newest and supposedly final report in the extended, "Gulf War and Health," series under VA contract as directed by the 1998 legislation. Entitled, "Gulf War and Health, Volume 10: Update of Health Effects of Serving in the Gulf War, 2016," it is highly problematic. While IOM's Volume 10 acknowledged that Gulf War illness is the signature adverse health outcome of the 1991 Gulf War - a fact that has been known by Gulf War veterans since the early 1990s and definitively shown by science since at least 2004 - its research and treatment recommendations range from disappointing to potentially damaging to the health and lives of Gulf War veterans with Gulf War Illness.

IOM's Volume 10 recommends no further research using animal models of Gulf War toxic exposures (p. 251). While the IOM Volume 10 panel acknowledged that an animal model would be advantageous for identifying and evaluating Gulf War Illness treatment strategies, they then suggested that the precise frequency, duration, dose of Gulf War exposures must be known in order to do so. This amounts to "rolling up the sidewalk" on this promising avenue of Gulf War Illness research, just when it is beginning to unravel the underlying biological mechanisms of Gulf War illness and point to treatment targets.

Past IOM review panels have been limited by VA's systemic failures in monitoring, assessing, and reporting the incidence and prevalence of health symptoms and diagnosed diseases in Gulf War (and other cohorts of) veterans. The IOM Volume 10 panel was similarly limited. As one example, IOM's Volume 10 report reads, "Because cancer incidence in the last 10 years has not been reported [by VA], additional follow-up is needed." (p.102). IOM's Volume 10 panel was tasked with reviewing published medical literature since the last major review six years ago, but due to one of VA's many failures couldn't do so because this new data hasn't been reported by VA.

However, unlike the panel's recommendation for additional follow-up with cancer incidence, IOM's Volume 10 committee instead inflicted damage when they recommended that, "further studies to assess the increased incidence and prevalence of circulatory, hematologic, musculoskeletal, gastrointestinal, genitourinary, reproductive, endocrine and metabolic, respiratory, chronic skin, and mental health conditions due to deployment in the Gulf War should not be undertaken" (pp. 9–10). Unlike IOM panels that are limited by VA's "don't look, don't find" failures, we must not mistake absence of VA evidence for evidence of absence of long histories of these adverse health outcomes in Gulf War veterans.

Like the earlier IOM reports, the Volume 10 panel found no new associations between Gulf War exposures and adverse health outcomes. It also found no new associations between Gulf War service and ill health.

While recommending greater effort towards treatment and acknowledging Gulf War Illness as the signature condition of the 1991 Gulf War, it recommended that research and treatment for Gulf War Illness now focus on, "brain-body interconnectedness." It also suggests focusing on "management" of Gulf War Illness. Together, these are an apparent departure from the optimism of the 2010 IOM report, which said, "effective treatments, cures, and, it is hoped, preventions . can likely be found."

The promising new science that is providing keys to Gulf War Illness's underlying mechanism and promising avenues towards treatment hasn't shifted course since 2010, it has just provided even greater evidence for the role of toxic exposures in Gulf War Illness and provided increasing detail in closing in on effective treatments. What has changed, however is that the IOM Volume 10 panel and reviewers included some of the same people and the same mindsets as the dark days of the 1990's, when everything about Gulf War veterans' exposures and symptoms was characterized as utterly unknowable, when Gulf War veterans' health issues were marginalized, and when VA and DOD officials seemed intent on restricting Gulf War Illness discussions to "stress" causation and mental health management rather than focusing on evidence-based treatments for Gulf War veterans' toxic wounds.

Those VA and DOD officials denied Gulf War veterans' toxic exposures, failed to develop treatments or preventions, redirected Gulf War veterans away from the goal of real healthcare, shut down research, and denied benefits. This new IOM recommendation amounts to little more than the same tired old themes from the 1990's - again, just when Gulf War Illness treatment research is finally making real progress to understand the illness and identify treatments

As I walked through the airport headed home following the meeting where this latest IOM report was released, my shoulder was heavy with a bag full of past IOM Gulf War reports. My heart was even heavier. Twenty-five years after our war, and nearly two decades after the enactment of the 1998 laws, these IOM Gulf War reports nearly fill a small shelf. But despite millions of dollars and countless panel members' work, the collective weight of these volumes have not associated animal exposures with human health outcomes, have found precious few health outcomes associated with Gulf War service, have not evaluated many of the exposures listed in the 1998 laws, and have added little toward the development of effective, evidence-based treatments for Gulf War Illness. Together, the IOM and its VA taskmaster have had little impact in improving the health or lives of Gulf War veterans with Gulf War Illness or achieving the goals set forth in the 1998 Gulf War legislation.

VA/DOD CLINICAL PRACTICE GUIDELINE (CPG)

As if the massive, multi-volume failure of Gulf War veterans wasn't enough, VA and DoD have now developed a highly problematic Clinical Practice Guideline for Gulf War Illness that goes back to the darkest days of the 1990s. In this Guideline, VA and DOD lump Gulf War Illness together with psychosomatic and other conditions that together, its authors call, "Chronic Multisymptom Illness" (CMI). It is worth noting that CMI is an overly broad and inappropriate catch-all label that IOM panels have rightly told VA to stop using for Gulf War Illness.

This Clinical Practice Guideline is intended for all healthcare providers - DOD, VA, and beyond. Its primary treatment recommendations for GWI are cognitive behavioral therapy (CBT), exercise, and psychotropic drugs. Suicidal ideation is listed in the Guide as a known "notable adverse effect" for every single one of those medications.

Despite public statements by VA officials, including before this Committee, that Gulf War Illness is not a psychological, psychiatric, or psychosomatic condition, this VA–DoD guide specifically compares "CMI" with a group of, "similar 'overlapping' symptom syndromes" and "somatization disorder". The terms "somatization disorder", and use the terms "somatization", "somatization disorder", "somatoform", and "somatoform disorder", and "psychosomatic" a stunning 52 times in the guide. The term, "hypochondriasis" is also used and referenced.

While the Clinical Practice Guideline authors use the term, "evidence-based", 19 times throughout the document in an apparent attempt to increase its credibility, they go on to state, "treatment of CMI is as much an art as it is a science" (p.8).

Showing its failure to rely on scientific evidence, a growing body of promising scientific research related to inflammatory cytokines, mitochondria and mitochondrial dysfunction (for example), including Coenzyme Q10 as a potential therapy. Yet, the term "cytokine" and variants appear only twice, and no reference whatsoever is made to mitochondria or word variants.

It would seem hard to believe, given the large body of peer-reviewed science on Gulf War Illness that has been published in more recent years, that a DOD or VA clinical guideline produced in 2014 would rely on the old "psychosomatic" fictions of the 1990s or on the VA and DOD officials that championed them. What's not surprising, however, is that the list of people who developed this guide that relies on psychosomatic artfulness rather than evidence-based treatments included some of the same old names from the dark days of the 1990s.

This guide is another example of VA's systemic research failures. From, "Don't look, don't find," to a renewed reliance on psychosomatic explanations and "treatments" for Gulf War Illness, the intent of the 1998 laws remain out of reach at VA past and present.

GULF WAR ILLNESS CDMRP

As many of the members of this Committee know, despite the serious problems noted above, there is a great deal of encouragement and hope for ill Gulf War veterans in the science being conducted and published in recent years. Much of this promising new research is in the treatment-focused Gulf War Illness Congressionally Directed Medical Research Program (CDMRP), which exists outside VA or the rest of DoD thanks to Congress, including many of the Members on this Committee.

One-third of the studies funded through this program are testing treatments that might help improve the health and lives of veterans with GWI. Two-thirds of the studies are aimed at Gulf War Illness's underlying mechanisms, including critically important animal studies that test exposures and measure health outcomes, identify treatment targets, and test treatments.

Three CDMRP-funded treatment studies have already shown promise in reducing certain GWI symptoms, including Coenzyme Q10, Carnosine, and acupuncture. Others have found powerful links between Gulf War toxic exposures and adverse health outcomes and are helping pave the way for treatment development.

The vast majority of this research is still in the pipeline. However, this powerfully encouraging progress could be at risk, by the IOM Volume 10 recommendations and by another IOM panel aimed at all the CDMRPs that is chaired and directed by some of the same former VA and DOD officials of the 1990s who have done so much harm to Gulf War veterans.

CONCLUSIONS

If we measure VA's success by how it has improved Gulf War veterans' health twenty-five years after the war, VA still has no evidence-based treatments for Gulf War Illness. VA has circumvented or ignored most of the aims of the 1998 laws. Instead, some of those same old VA and DOD officials from the dark days of the 1990s have joined together in their usual old cabal and are once again pushing long-discredited theories of psychosomatic causation and "treatment" in new and potentially influential ways.

In twenty-five years, VA has made little progress on Gulf War Illness, and now appears to be working to roll back the clock to the dark days of the 1990's.

□ Instead of following recommendations on Gulf War Illness research that would lead to improving ill Gulf War veterans' health and lives, VA eliminated the Research Advisory Committee's (RAC) ability to evaluate the effectiveness of all federal Gulf War research efforts, limited its scope from all federal research to just VA's, eliminated its treatment focus mandate, and more.

□ VA admitted to "losing" its registry for Gulf War spouses and children. It is unclear what VA has done to recover that data.

□ VA continues make reports to Congress that inflate "Gulf War research" spending by including studies that are not specific to Gulf War veterans.

□ VA has the authority to develop new presumptives for these ill and suffering veterans, but unlike with Agent Orange, has failed to identify any new conditions beyond a set of rare endemic infectious diseases that affect almost no one.

□ IOM's latest report, shaped by VA's contract, argues that individual Gulf War exposures are forever unknowable. We knew that when seeking the 1998 legislation, aimed at connecting generic exposure data with health outcomes. VA has stymied those efforts.

□ VA has not linked a single adverse health outcome to any Gulf War exposures nor created a single new presumptive condition under the 1998 laws to help suffering veterans beyond the largely irrelevant endemic infections noted earlier.

Twenty-five years later, one-fourth to one-third of us Gulf War veterans continue to struggle with the health and life effects of Gulf War Illness. Others among us have died of ALS, brain cancer, other diseases, suicide. Yet VA, with the aid of DoD and the complicity of the IOM, has made little progress in developing evidence-based treatments or improving the health and lives of veterans suffering from signature injury of the 1991 Gulf War - Gulf War Illness.

Twenty-five years later, one-fourth to one-third of us continues to battle the signature injury of the 1991 Gulf War: Gulf War Illness. Others among us have died of ALS, brain cancer, other diseases, suicide. Yet VA, with the aid of DoD and the complicity of the IOM, has made little progress in developing evidence-based treatments or improving the health and lives of veterans suffering from signature injury of the 1991 Gulf War - Gulf War Illness.

Twenty-five years later, ill Gulf War veterans are still in pain. They are suffering. They have been begging for help for years and years. Twenty-five years later, Gulf War veterans are battling against VA and DOD bureaucrats, including some of the very same ones who fought against the 1998 laws in the first place.

We must not continue to allow VA and DoD to substitute "risk communication" for evidence-based healthcare, psychosomatic drugs for treatment-focused research, spin for substance, or "Don't look, don't find" for the objective collection, analysis, and reporting of deployment health outcomes. The letter, the spirit, and the intent of the 1998 Persian Gulf War laws have yet to be achieved.

On this 25th anniversary of the war, our Gulf War veterans deserve the best that modern science and the U.S. government can offer to improve their health and lives.

Mr. Chairman, as one of us Gulf War veteran, and Members of this powerful Committee, please join together with your colleagues on both sides of the aisle and in both houses and help fix these serious issues, once and for all.

Statements For The Record

LUNG CANCER ALLIANCE

Lung Cancer Alliance (LCA) thanks the chairman and the committee for allowing the submission of the following comments for the record of this hearing.

LCA, the leading national lung cancer policy, advocacy and patient support organization, is deeply concerned by the lack of updated disease specific incidence and mortality data from the Department of Veterans Affairs in the Gulf War and Health Volume 10 Report.

Without this critical information, the Vol. 10 report, perforce, had to conclude:

"...that there is insufficient/ adequate evidence to determine whether an association exists between deployment to the Gulf War and any form of cancer, including lung cancer and brain cancer."

The Vol.8 report indicated that at that point in time, only lung cancer showed a statistically relevant excess between Gulf War deployed veterans and non-deployed veterans, based on a published 2010 study by Young et al which linked Defense Manpower Data Center datasets with files from 28 state cancer registries and the Department of Veterans Affairs Central Cancer Registry.

The study concluded that the 15% excess of lung cancer diagnoses in deployed veterans over the years 1991–2006 warranted additional follow-up studies. Indeed, the Vol.10 report concluded that additional follow-up was necessary.

The Vol.10 report gives no indication that this was done. In fact, on page 102, the Vol. 10 Report states:

Because cancer incidence in the past 10 years has not been reported, additional follow-up is needed.

Many cancers have long latency periods, 20–30 years in the case of lung cancer as both Vol. 8 and 10 accurately report. The median age for a cancer diagnosis in the United States is 65 (70 for lung cancer) and the median age of Gulf War veterans in 1991 was 28. Thus, the impact of Gulf War deployment on cancer incidence and mortality cannot be accurately evaluated without long term follow-up and accurate incidence and mortality statistics.

Updating the 2010 Young study would have been the most logical, cost-effective and statistically significant resource in preparing for Vol.10.

The only other Primary study cited in Vol.10 was the 2015 update (Sim et al.) on the Australian Gulf War veterans which did not show elevated cancer incidence or mortality rates. However, while the survey included all 1,871 Australia Gulf war veterans, 84% were Navy, not deployed ground forces, and 87% were under the age of 55 at the time of the update.

The Vol. 10 report conceded that telephone/web surveys of U.S. Gulf War veterans by committee member (Dursa et al., 2015) and the VA showing no disparity of impact did not qualify as primary studies and were not sufficiently powered or cross-checked with actual mortality and incidence data to be considered statistically significant.

When queried by LCA, the committee staff indicated that they did not ask the VA for disease-specific mortality data. Clearly this has to be done.

Lung cancer is the leading cause of all cancer deaths. Its annual mortality is equivalent to all deaths from breast, prostate, colon and pancreatic cancers combined. Veterans, especially those who served in combat, are at highest risk due to the combination of smoking rates and exposure to carcinogens.

CT screening for a defined high risk population ages 55–80 has been validated by one of the largest randomized controlled trials ever carried out by the National Cancer Institute, given a B recommendation by the U.S. Preventive Services Task Force, a required preventive service covered by commercial insurance and Medicare with no co-pays, deductibles or co-insurance.

Yet the VA , whose population is at highest risk, still refuses to implement this life-saving benefit system-wide.

Since the median age of Gulf War veterans is now the mid-50's, LCA would urge the committee to require the VA to immediately implement CT lung cancer screening. Indeed, CT screening will provide more concrete and accurate data on lung cancer, as well as data on heart disease and other lung diseases, than the $500,000,000, 18-year Gulf War study has to date.

☞

NATIONAL GULF WAR RESOURCE CENTER

STATEMENT FOR THE RECORD OF RONALD E. BROWN, GULF WAR VETERAN & PRESIDENT, NATIONAL GULF WAR RESOURCE CENTER

Thank you, Chairman Coffman, Ranking Member Kuster, and Members of the House Veterans' Affairs Subcommittee on Oversight and Investigations. I thank you for holding this investigative hearing on Gulf War health issues on the eve of the 25th anniversary of our successful ground invasion to liberate Kuwait.

My name is Ronald Brown; I'm President of the National Gulf War Resource Center (NGWRC). The NGWRC is a small 501 (c) (3) non-profit veteran service organization, which is comprised of sick Persian Gulf War veterans who volunteer our time to advocate for our fellow veterans suffering from the complexities of modern warfare. We specialize in Gulf War Illness claims, we work with veterans to educate and assist them in the claims process. We also work with policy makers inside the VA, in an attempt to accomplish two goals: first, to insure clinicians are better trained about conditions facing this group of veterans to insure the veterans receive the best health care possible.

Secondly, we are working to address and correct issues affecting this group of veterans, such as the high denial rate of Gulf War illness related claims.

We also strive to inform veterans concerning ongoing research being conducted by both the Department of Veterans Affairs and the Congressionally Directed Medical Research Programs (CDMRP). We strive to get veterans involved in the research as participants.

In my view, the Congressionally Directed Medical Research Program (CDMRP) is by far leading the way on research for our sick Gulf War veterans. Many studies funded by the CDMRP have shown promise that may provide insight into Gulf War illness.These studies may eventually identify ways to diagnose and treat Gulf War Illness. Additional follow-up (replication on a larger scale) is needed on these promising pilot studies. Unfortunately, in our view, the VA Office of Research and Development (ORD) have been slow to replicate any of these promising pilot studies. Until this is done, these studies will not benefit veterans by providing effective treatments or new presumptive conditions for benefits.

Recently, I attended the public briefing for The Gulf War and Health, Volume 10: Update of Health Effects of Serving in the Gulf War. While I agree with the committee's recommendation to use the term Gulf War Illness (GWI), overall I was shocked and troubled by the conclusions and recommendations this committee reached.

This committee suggest that the "conditions associated with Gulf War deployment are primarily mental health disorders and functional medical disorders and that these associations emphasize the interconnectedness of the brain and body (page 11, IOM vol 10)." This committee also stated "Veterans who were deployed to the Gulf War do not appear to have an increased risk for many long term health conditions with the exceptions of Post-Traumatic Stress Disorder (PTSD), Gulf War Illness (GWI), Chronic Fatigue Syndrome (CFS), Functional Gastrointestinal conditions, generalized anxiety disorder, depression and substance abuse."

The committee added further insult to sick Desert Storm veterans when they recommended: "Further studies to assess the increased incidence and prevalence of circulatory, hematologic, musculoskeletal, gastrointestinal, genitourinary, reproductive, endocrine and metabolic, respiratory, chronic skin, and mental health conditions due to deployment in the Gulf War should not be undertaken. Rather, future research related to these conditions should focus on ensuring that Gulf War veterans receive timely and effective treatment (page 9, IOM vol 10)." This committee recommended that future research should focus on treating and managing Gulf War illness rather than its causes.

I agree treatments and managing Gulf War illness is important; however, I also believe that we should understand the causes of this illness in Desert Storm veterans if we are to prevent toxic illness and injury to future generations of our Armed forces. This committee recommended individual and environmental biomonitoring during future conflicts. I agree with this recommendation with skepticism based on DOD's history of reluctance to release information concerning exposures during Desert Storm.

I strongly disagree with this committee's recommendation that "further studies to assess the increased incidence and prevalence of health conditions due to deployment in the Gulf War should not be undertaken." If this committee has their way, I'm afraid we never will learn what caused our illness, how to treat ill Persian Gulf Veterans, and we will never have the evidence to warrant adding new presumptive conditions.

Since 2002, sick Desert Storm veterans who have attended, or listen in by phone, to the Research Advisory Committee (RAC) meetings have listened to presentations that show VA epidemiological studies have shown that deployed Desert Storm veterans have higher prevalence of:

- Migraine headaches (20.3% deployed vs 16.1% non-deployed).
- Chronic obstructive pulmonary disease (8.4% deployed vs 6.3% non-deployed).
- Dermatitis (27.4% deployed vs 21.1% non-deployed).
- Functional dyspepsia (27.7% deployed vs 15.9% non-deployed).
- Tachycardia (8.1% deployed vs 5.9% non-deployed).
- Irritable bowel syndrome (24.4% deployed vs 14.3% non- deployed).

Yet, the IOM committee puts many of these issues listed above in its Inadequate/Insufficient Evidence to Determine Whether an Association Exist category.

There is most definitely a problem with this committee's report as the VA's own research shows one thing, and the IOM committee is saying something completely different. This report is an injustice to sick Desert Storm veterans. This report winds the clock backwards to the 1994 mindset. In 1994 the VA as well as the Department of Defense (DOD) said that GWI was nothing more than combat stress, PTSD, or psychological illnesses. Desert Storm veterans thought we had escaped the "it's all in your head" mindset with the ground breaking 2008 Research Advisory Committee report. Yet here we are twenty-five years after the war, and sick Desert Storm veterans are still waiting for treatments, many are still waiting on service connection for presumptive conditions per current law, and we still wait and hope new presumptive conditions will be added.

My reasoning for my belief that there is a problem with this committee's report is during the briefing when I asked why studies that showed cancer at higher rates weren't considered by this committee, URMC Professor Deborah Cory-Slechta referenced the 2004 GOA report that stated the Khamisiyah plume model was flawed that was used in VA's research. This same GOA report also stated that the VA and DOD's hospital rate study was also flawed, yet this committee still used this study to reach their conclusions (page 200, IOM vol 10).

This IOM committee retrieved over 280 studies of potential relevance to this report. 204 studies that "did not appear to have immediate relevance, based on an assessment of the title and abstract" were deleted without consideration leaving only 76 potential relevant studies considered and discussed by this committee (page 25, IOM vol 10). Nowhere in this report are these 204 deleted studies listed. My question is how many of these deleted studies were VA and CDMRP studies? An additional 100 papers dealing with animal models were reviewed and half were deleted for further consideration (page 26, IOM vol 10). Of the half that was not considered, how many were VA and CDMRP papers?

The NGWRC honestly feels this report is flawed. We are grateful that the House Veterans' Affairs Subcommittee on Oversite and Investigation has decided to investigate this matter.

Recommendations:

(1). Ensure any future contract between the VA and IOM is made public for Desert Storm veterans. This would ensure transparency.

(2). To further ensure transparency Veterans Service Organizations (VSO) should be invited to the IOM's briefing to the Department of Veterans Affairs.

(3). Veterans Service Organizations should receive a copy of future IOM reports prior to the public briefing. This will allow the VSOs to form reasonable questions for the committee.

(4). Ensure the IOM committee list all studies they deem not relevant in its report. A reasonable explanation as to why the study was found irrelevant should be provided. This would ensure researchers knowledge of the IOM's definition of "immediate relevance".

(5). Desert Storm veterans and our researchers need help in regards to replication on a larger scale of studies that have shown promise. Unfortunately, the VA Office of Research and Development (ORD) have been slow to replicate any of these promising pilot studies. If the VA is unable to replicate this amazing and promising research, then perhaps increased funding should be provided to the CDMRP to replicate these promising studies on a larger scale. Until this is done, these small promising pilot studies will not benefit veterans by providing effective treatments or new presumptive conditions for benefits.

Respectfully,
Ronald E. Brown President
National Gulf War Resource Center

☛

JAMES BINNS

With respect to Gulf War veterans' health, VA pays no more attention to Congress than it does to science. As described below, Congress has ordered report after report from the Institute of Medicine (IOM), specifying in law the work to be done. However, VA has consistently failed to contract for what Congress actually ordered. The IOM has been a willing accomplice, changing its own standards of evidence and appointing biased committees to accommodate VA's purposes. As a result, the reports inevitably produce conclusions that deny any connection between toxic exposures and the shattered health of Gulf War veterans, and promote the discredited 1990's VA position that their illness is largely psychiatric.

These same corrupt practices have been employed to deny the effect of toxic exposures from burn pits on the health of recent Iraq and Afghanistan veterans.

1. Public Laws 105–277 and 105–368, enacted in 1998, are the foundation for the IOM Gulf War and Health reports. Congress required VA to contract with the IOM to evaluate the health risks of thirty-three toxic substances and medications to which troops were exposed in the war. The law required consideration of animal studies because most studies of the effects of toxic substances are necessarily done in animals.

But VA did not contract for consideration of animal studies, and the IOM actually changed its standards of evidence to exclude animal studies - the exact opposite of what Congress ordered. As a result, these studies - the basic studies that show these toxic substances are toxic—have never been considered in any IOM report, and no IOM report has ever found sufficient evidence that any of the thirty-three toxic agents are associated with health problems.

The entire IOM Gulf War series of reports is a house of cards, as detailed in Appendix A.

These same corrupt practices have been employed to deny the effect of toxic exposures from burn pits on the health of recent Iraq and Afghanistan veterans. (below, pp. 12–13)

2. In 2010, in Public Law 111–275, Congress required VA to contract with the IOM for a "comprehensive review of the best treatments for chronic multisymptom illness in Gulf War veterans."

The statute directed that the IOM "shall convene a group of medical professionals who are experienced in treating [Gulf War veterans] who have been diagnosed with chronic multisymptom illness or another health condition related to chemical and environmental exposures . . ." [1]

VA ignored this direction and instead contracted with the IOM for a literature review of largely psychiatric diseases by a committee with no experience in treating Gulf War veterans, heavily weighted with specialists in psychosomatic medicine and stress. [2] Rather than capturing the valuable treatment experience of Gulf War veterans' doctors, as Congress intended, the resulting 2013 IOM treatment report was a restatement of government fictions from the 1990's, foreshadowing the 2016 IOM report and the new VA/DoD Clinical Practice Guideline.

3. In 2008, Congress enacted Public Law 110–389 requiring VA to contract with the IOM "to conduct a comprehensive epidemiological study . [to] identify the incidence and prevalence of diagnosed neurological diseases, including multiple sclerosis, Parkinson's disease, and brain cancers . . ." in 1991 Gulf War veterans, Post-9/11 Global Operations veterans, and non-deployed comparison groups. [3]

For seven years, VA refused to contract for the study, despite repeated urging by the Research Advisory Committee on Gulf War Veterans Illnesses. [4] In 2015, VA fi-

---

[1] Veterans Benefits Act of 2010, Sec. 805, http://library.clerk.house.gov/reference-files/PPL—111—275—VeteransBenefitsAct—2010.pdf

[2] http://www.scribd.com/doc/150949964/WHITE–PAPER–IOM–CMI–Panel-Membership-Analysis

[3] Public Law 110–389, Section 804

[4] http://www.va.gov/RAC–GWVI/docs/Committee—Documents/CommitteeDocJune2012.pdf (Appendix E)

nally contracted with the IOM, but wrote in the contract that the IOM could only use VA data. The IOM committee declined to proceed with the study because the VA data was insufficient for a rigorous study.[5]

In the absence of the study ordered by Congress in 2008, the 2016 report found the evidence insufficient to reach conclusions that these conditions are associated with Gulf War service.[6]

4. The membership of IOM Gulf War report committees has usually been biased toward VA's discredited position, including the 2016 committee.

See the November 2014 letter to Dr. Victor Dzau, president of the IOM, attached as Appendix B below (pp. 37–42), objecting to the makeup of the 2016 Gulf War and Health committee. "[T]he membership is grossly imbalanced toward the 1990's government position that Gulf War veterans have no special health problem - just what happens after every war, related to psychiatric issues, and not environmental exposures."

The letter documented that eight the members of the committee were associated with the 1990's government position, including the former 1990's VA Undersecretary for Health, Dr. Kenneth Kizer, who was the chief advocate for the position. Eight members were neutral. Subsequent to the letter, one neutral member resigned and one individual with current Gulf War research experience was added, the only person on the committee with such experience.

The last two pages of the letter analyze the 2016 committee membership. (below, pp. 45–46)

The letter predicted that: "Reviving this discredited fiction will cause veterans' doctors to prescribe inappropriate psychiatric medications, and will misdirect research to find effective treatments down blind alleys - an unconscionable breach of the duty owed to veterans and expected of the Institute of Medicine. "

APPENDIX A

VA AND IOM COLLABORATION TO EXCLUDE CONSIDERATION OF ANIMAL STUDIES

REQUIRED BY LAW

Public Laws 105–277 and 105–368 are the foundation for the Institute of Medicine (IOM) Gulf War and Health reports. Congress required VA to contract with the IOM to evaluate the health risks of thirty-three toxic substances and medications to which troops were exposed in the war. The law required consideration of animal studies on a par with human studies because most studies of toxic substances are necessarily done in animals for ethical reasons.

But VA did not contract for consideration of animal studies, and the IOM actually changed its standards of evidence to exclude animal studies - the exact opposite of what Congress ordered. As a result, these studies - the basic studies that show these toxic substances are toxic—have never been considered in any IOM report, and no IOM report has ever found sufficient evidence that any of the thirty-three listed toxic agents are associated with health problems.

Consider, for example, the twenty-three animal studies on pages 160–161 of the 2008 report of the Research Advisory Committee on Gulf War Veterans Illnesses, showing that low levels of nerve gas, below the level that causes symptoms at the time of exposure, cause long-term adverse health effects, contrary to what was believed at the time of the war. Because of these studies, an update report on the effects of sarin was ordered from the IOM, but as described below, VA and IOM staff conspired to ensure that the report would not consider animal studies in its conclusions, even though new animal studies were the only reason for ordering the report. http://www.va.gov/RAC–GWVI/docs/Committee—Documents/GWIandHealthofGWVeterans—RAC–GWVIReport—2008.pdf

The entire IOM Gulf War series of reports is a house of cards, as detailed below.

These same corrupt practices have been employed to deny the effect of toxic exposures from burn pits on the health of recent Iraq and Afghanistan veterans. (below, pp. 12–13)

* * *

These 1998 statutes required the IOM to identify illnesses experienced by Armed Forces members who served in the war, "including diagnosed illnesses and undiagnosed illnesses" (the term then used for what is now called "Gulf War Ill-

---

[5] http://iom.nationalacademies.org/Reports/2015/Considerations-for-Designing-Epidemiologic-Study-for-Multiple-Sclerosis-and-other-Neurological-disorders-Veterans.aspx
[6] 2016 IOM Gulf War and Health report, pp. 102,145,149.

ness"). The statutes then asked, for each of the thirty-three agents and each illness, "whether a statistical association exists between exposure to an agent . . . and an increased risk of illness in human or animal populations."

Congress required consideration of studies in animals because most studies of toxic substances and drugs are necessarily done in animals for ethical reasons. It did not ask for information on how much of an agent Gulf War troops were exposed to. It was well known that no such information exists.

These basic animal studies have never been considered in any IOM report. The 2016 report discusses some animal studies involving exposures to combinations of agents, but it acknowledges that "studies examining single exposures are not considered here" because "[e]arly volumes of the Gulf War and Health series described animal studies . . . on the association between exposure to a single toxicant and the health outcomes that may result. . ."

2016 IOM Gulf War and Health report, Vol. 10, p. 239

But the earlier IOM reports make clear they did not consider these animal studies in their conclusions. The chairman of the 2016 committee, Dr. Deborah Cory-Slechta, was a member of the committee for the 2003 IOM Gulf War report on Insecticides and Solvents, so she is familiar with the procedures used. While the 2003 report "described" numerous animal studies, it admitted that "animal studies had a limited role in the committee's assessment between exposure and a health outcome. Animal data . . . were not used as part of the weight-of-evidence . . ."

2003 IOM Gulf War and Health report, Vol. 2, p. 3

The same admission can be found in every IOM Gulf War report on the health effects of toxic substances. Thus, the 2016 report did not consider these basic animal studies in their conclusions, relying on the earlier reports, but the earlier reports didn't consider them either. As a result, since most studies of toxic exposures are done in animals, no IOM report has ever found sufficient evidence that any of the thirty-three listed toxic exposures and medications are associated with adverse health outcomes.

The whole IOM Gulf War series of reports is a house of cards.

In her preface to the 2016 report, Dr. Cory-Slechta points to the "ever unknowable impact of the various chemical exposures that occurred. . .", because "[o]bjective exposure data gathered during and after the war have been, and are expected to continue to be, unavailable." 2016 IOM Gulf War and Health report, Vol. 10, p. ix

But Congress never asked for consideration of exposure data. It was well known that data did not exist. What it did ask for was consideration of animal data. But it has never gotten it. It has never gotten it because VA did not contract for the reports that Congress ordered.

The IOM has been a willing collaborator in this deceit, changing its own standards of evidence to exclude animal studies - exactly the opposite action from what the law required.

It made this change quietly, and has deceitfully implied that nothing changed. As presented in the 2003 report, "[t]he committee used the [standards of evidence] from previous IOM studies because they have gained wide acceptance over more than a decade by Congress, government agencies, researchers, and veterans groups." "The [standards of evidence] closely resemble those used by . . . IOM committees that have evaluated . . . herbicides used in Vietnam." 2003 IOM Gulf War and Health report, Vol. 2, p. 3

(See the similar language on p. 3 of the 2016 report.)

In fact, however, the standards were subtly changed from the Agent Orange standards to exclude consideration of animal studies. Animal studies are discussed in the Gulf War reports, but when it comes to arriving at the reports' conclusions, they are not considered, applying the doctored standards of evidence (what the IOM calls the "categories of association").

For sixteen years, VA, DoD, and IOM staff have manipulated IOM Gulf War reports on the health effects of veterans' toxic exposures. As a result, the reports have consistently found "insufficient evidence" that the exposures are associated with illness, leading to VA determinations that the illness does not qualify for benefits as service-connected. Of equal importance, these dishonest reports have also misled researchers seeking to understand the causes of Gulf War illness in order to identify treatments to improve veterans' health and preventive measures to protect future US forces.

In recent years, the same techniques have been applied to IOM reports on the health effects of toxic substances released by burn pits on recent Iraq and Afghanistan veterans.

The balance of this Appendix will review in detail these corrupt practices.

1. The governing statute expressly requires consideration of animal studies.

In PL 105–277 and PL 105–368, Congress in 1998 directed the Department of Veterans Affairs to contract with the National Academy of Sciences (NAS, the parent organization of the Institute of Medicine, IOM), to review the scientific literature regarding substances to which troops were exposed in the 1991 Gulf War to determine if these substances are associated with an increased risk of illness. These reports were to be used by the Secretary of Veterans Affairs in determining whether the illness should be presumed service-connected for the purpose of veterans' benefits.

The law directed the NAS (IOM) to identify the "biological, chemical, or other toxic agents, environmental or wartime hazards, or preventive medicines or vaccines" to which members of the Armed Forces may have been exposed during the war. 38 USC Sec. 1117, note Sec. 1603 (c). [attached to this Appendix below at p. 14] The law listed thirty-three specific "toxic agents, environmental or wartime hazards, or preventive medicines or vaccines associated with Gulf War service" to be considered, including various pesticides; pyridostigmine bromide, a drug used as a nerve agent prophylaxis; low-level nerve agents; other chemicals, metals, sources of radiation; and infectious diseases. 38 USC Sec. 1117, note Sec. 1603 (a), (d). [below, pp. 15–16] The law further required the NAS (IOM) to identify illnesses, "including diagnosed illnesses and undiagnosed illnesses," experienced by Armed Forces members who served in the war. 38 USC Sec. 1117, note Sec. 1603 (c) [below, p. 14]

"For each agent, hazard, or medicine or vaccine and illness identified," the law provided that:

"The National Academy of Sciences shall determine .

(A) whether a statistical association exists between exposure to the agent . and the illness . . .

(B) the increased risk of the illness among human or animal populations exposed to the agent . and

(C) whether a plausible biological mechanism or other evidence of a causal relationship exists ."

38 USC Sec. 1117, note Sec. 1603 (e) [below, p. 16, emphasis added]

The statute went on to provide that the Secretary of Veterans Affairs should consider both human and animal studies in determining whether a presumption of service connection is warranted. He was to consider "the exposure in humans or animals" to an agent and "the occurrence of a diagnosed or undiagnosed illness in humans or animals."

38 USC Sec. 1118 (b)(1)(B) [below, p. 21, emphasis added]

Congress thus expressly required consideration of animal as well as human studies by both the National Academy of Sciences (the Institute of Medicine) and the Secretary of Veterans Affairs. This statutory requirement reflects the fact that most studies on the biological effects of hazardous substances are necessarily done in animals, for ethical reasons. Consider, for example, the twenty-three studies on the long-term effects of low level sarin exposure, or the eighteen studies evaluating the combined effects of pyridostigmine bromide, pesticides and insect repellant listed on pages 160–161 and 170–171 of the 2008 Research Advisory Committee on Gulf War Veterans Illnesses report, all of which were done in animals. http://www.va.gov/RAC—GWVI/docs/Committee—Documents/GWIandHealthofGWVeterans—RAC—GWVIReport—2008.pdf

When the first IOM report was conducted under the law, however, animal studies were omitted from the standard for determining whether an association exists between an exposure and a health effect. The report states:

"For its evaluation and categorization of the degree of association between each exposure and a human health effect, however, the [IOM] committee only used evidence from human studies."

Gulf War and Health, Volume 1, (2000), p. 72 [below, p. 23]

Considering only human studies, and not the much larger relevant literature on animal studies, the IOM committees have never found sufficient evidence of an association for the exposures and illnesses experienced by Gulf War veterans. Following the reports of the IOM, the Secretary of Veterans Affairs has made no determinations of service-connection for these exposures and illnesses for veterans' benefits. (VA asserts that it covers Gulf War veterans on other grounds for their "undiagnosed illnesses," but VA statistics show that over 80% of such veterans' claims are denied. http://www.scribd.com/doc/241661207/Binns-Parting-Thoughts-093014)

This pattern has been followed in all IOM Gulf War reports to date. More recently, it has been applied to IOM reports on the effects of toxic exposures fromburn pits on the health of recent Iraq and Afghanistan veterans.

2. The exclusion of animal studies was deliberate.

A close examination of what occurred makes clear that the exclusion of animal studies was not an oversight. It was deliberate.

To express conclusions as to whether an association between an exposure and an illness exists, the first IOM Gulf report defined five standards of evidence, which it called the "Categories of Association." Gulf War and Health, Vol. 1, pp. 83–84. [below, pp. 25–26] The same categories have been used in all subsequent IOM Gulf War exposure reports:

- Sufficient Evidence of a Causal Relationship
- Sufficient Evidence of an Association
- Limited/Suggestive Evidence of an Association
- Inadequate/Insufficient Evidence to Determine Whether an Association Does or Does Not Exist
- Limited/Suggestive Evidence of No Association.

Each substance was ranked according to these categories. How a substance is ranked becomes the all-important conclusion of the report as to whether an association exists between an exposure and illness.

Where did these categories come from? The report explained: "The committee used the established categories of association from previous IOM studies, because they have gained wide acceptance for more than a decade by Congress, government agencies, researchers, and veteran groups." "The categories closely resemble those used by several IOM committees that evaluated .. herbicides used in Vietnam ." Gulf War and Health, Volume I, p. 83. [below, p. 25]

IOM Gulf War reports have repeatedly emphasized over the years that their methodology is based on the IOM Agent Orange reports. However, it is revealing to compare a category of association used in the Agent Orange reports with the same category used in the Gulf War reports.

Agent Orange:

"Sufficient Evidence of an Association. Evidence is sufficient to conclude that there is a positive association. That is, a positive association has been observed between herbicides and the outcome in studies in which chance, bias, and confounding could be ruled out ." Veterans and Agent Orange: 1996 Update, p. 97 [below, p. 27, emphasis added]

Gulf War:

"Sufficient Evidence of an Association. Evidence is sufficient to conclude that there is a positive association. That is, a positive association has been observed between an exposure to a specific agent and a health outcome in human studies in which chance, bias, and confounding could be ruled out . . ."
Gulf War and Health: Volume I, p. 83 [below, p. 25, emphasis added]

The Gulf War category does indeed "closely resemble" the Agent Orange category—with a conspicuous exception. The word "human" has been inserted in the Gulf War category. This addition obviously did not occur by accident. It was deliberate, as was the misleading language that these were the "established categories of association from previous IOM reports."

Thus, not only have the IOM Gulf War studies been conducted in violation of the direction Congress provided in the statute; this violation has been deliberate, with intent to conceal.

As to why it was done, one can speculate based on the knowledge that the Agent Orange language, just a few years earlier, had produced an IOM report that found that Agent Orange exposure was associated with cancer (after two decades of government denial of any health consequence). This finding led to a presumption of service connection for thousands of Vietnam veterans with cancer.

It should be noted that the IOM Gulf War reports state that animal studies were considered for purposes of "biological plausibility": "For its evaluation and categorization of the degree of association between each exposure and a human health effect, . the committee only used evidence from human studies. Nevertheless, the committee did use nonhuman studies as the basis for judgments about biological plausibility, which is one of the criteria for establishing causation." Gulf War and Health, Volume 1, p. 72 [below, p. 25]

The terms of the Gulf War categories of association make clear, however, that biological plausibility and causation only relate to the highest category of evidence, "sufficient evidence of a causal relationship," and are not considered unless there has been a previous finding of "sufficient evidence of association":

"Sufficient Evidence of a Causal Relationship. Evidence is sufficient to conclude that a causal relationship exists between the exposure to a specific agent and a health outcome in humans. The evidence fills the criteria for sufficient evidence of association (below) and satisfies several of the criteria used to assess causality:

strength of association, dose-response relationship, consistency of association, temporal relationship, specificity of association, and biological plausibility."

"Sufficient Evidence of an Association. Evidence is sufficient to conclude that there is a positive association. That is, a positive association has been observed between an exposure to a specific agent and a health outcome in human studies in which chance, bias, and confounding could be ruled out with reasonable confidence." Gulf War and Health, Volume 1, p. 83. [below, p. 25, emphasis added]

Thus, only if there has already been a finding of "sufficient evidence of association" do the issues of causality and biological plausibility arise, and a finding of "sufficient evidence of association" depends solely on human studies. Unless an association is found based on human studies, biological plausibility—and animal studies—are not considered.

It is notable that the statute does not require evidence of a "casual relationship" to trigger a presumption of service connection. It only requires evidence of a "positive association":

"[T]he Secretary shall prescribe regulations providing that a presumption of service connection is warranted [if the Secretary makes a] determination based on sound medical and scientific evidence that a positive association exists between——

(i) the exposure of humans or animals to a biological, chemical, or other toxic agent, environmental or wartime hazard, or preventive medicine or vaccine known or presumed to be associated with service in the Southwest Asia theater of operations during the Persian Gulf War; and
(ii) the occurrence of a diagnosed or undiagnosed illness in humans or animals." 38 USC Sec. 1118 (b)(1) [emphasis added, below pp. 20–21]

In short, in direct contravention of the law, the methodology established for the IOM Gulf War reports deliberately excluded animal studies from consideration as to whether an association exists between an exposure and an illness, the only question that matters in the determination of veterans' benefits.

3. VA and IOM staff privately collaborated to produce these results.

As to how this was done, the history of one of the IOM Gulf War reports provides an indication. The 2004 IOM Updated Literature Review of Sarin is the most egregious example of the distortion of science produced by excluding animal studies from the evidence considered in these reports' conclusions. In late 2002, a number of new studies on sarin nerve gas, sponsored by the Department of Defense, revealed that contrary to previous belief, low level exposures (below the level required to produce symptoms at the time of exposure) produced long-term effects on the nervous and immune systems. Naturally, these studies were done in animals, not humans.

A previous IOM report on sarin in 2000 had found insufficient evidence of an association between low-level sarin and long-term health effects based on scientific knowledge as of that date. On January 24, 2003, then-VA Secretary Anthony Principi wrote the president of the Institute of Medicine: "Recently, a number of new studies have been published on the effects of Sarin on laboratory animals." He asked the IOM to report back "on whether this new research affects earlier conclusions of IOM . . . about possible long-term health consequences of exposure to low levels of Sarin." [attached, p. 29]

In 2004, the IOM delivered its report. The Updated Literature Review of Sarin discussed the new animal studies in its text. However, true to form, the report did not consider animal studies in the all-important categories of association, even though the new animal studies were the only reason for doing the report.

"As with previous committees, this committee used animal data for making assessments of biological plausibility . rather than as part of the weight of evidence to determine the likelihood that an exposure to a specific agent might cause a long-term outcome." Updated Literature Review of Sarin (2004), p. 18 [below, p. 30] Accordingly, the report found insufficient evidence of an association.

To understand this bizarre outcome, it is revealing that following Secretary Principi's letter, an IOM proposal was prepared which became the basis for a contract between the IOM and VA.

The proposal for the sarin update was sent to VA on March 11, 2003, with a cover letter from Susanne Stoiber, executive director of the IOM, to Dr. Mark Brown, director of the VA Environmental Agents Service, part of the Office of Public Health. The cover letter stated: "This proposal follows a request from Secretary Anthony J. Principi and discussions with yourself requesting an update of the health effects of the chemical warfare agent sarin." [below, p. 31]

The proposal contained the following "Statement of Task": [below, p. 34]

"The committee will conduct a review of the peer-reviewed literature published since earlier IOM reports on health effects associated with exposure to sarin and related compounds. Relevant epidemiologic studies will be considered. With regard to the toxicological literature, the committee will generally use review articles to present a broad overview of the toxicology of sarin and to make assessments of biologic plausibility regarding the compound of study and health effects; individual toxicology research papers will be evaluated as warranted.

The committee will make determinations on the strength of the evidence for associations between sarin and human health effects. If published peer-reviewed information is available on the dose of sarin exposure in Gulf War veterans, the committee may address the potential health risks posed to the veterans . . . "

In other words, the Statement of Task established that the update report would use the same "categories of association" as the earlier Gulf War reports. The "determinations on the strength of the evidence" would be made on the basis of the "associations between sarin and human health effects". "With regard to the toxicological literature" (which included the new animal studies), its use would be confined to the assessment of "biological plausibility" to which animal studies had previously been relegated. Thus, the update report would exclude animal studies from its key conclusions, even though animal studies were the only reason for doing the report.

Moreover, the Statement of Task set up another fundamental constraint for the report. The IOM committee would be permitted to address the potential health risks posed to the veterans "[i]f published peer-reviewed information is available on the dose of sarin exposure in Gulf War veterans." As anyone familiar with Gulf War research would know, including Dr. Brown and his IOM counterparts, there is no published peer-reviewed information available on the dose of sarin exposure in Gulf War veterans, for the reason that no such information was collected during the war. As noted in the previous 2000 IOM report on sarin, "as discussed throughout this report, there is a paucity of data regarding the actual agents and doses to which individual veterans were exposed." Gulf War and Health, Volume 1, p. 84. [below, p. 26] In order for the IOM committee to address the health risks posed to veterans, it had to meet a condition that was impossible to meet.

These constraints in the Statement of Task were not contained in the letter from Secretary Principi requesting the report. (To the contrary, they appear to contradict it.) They must have come from the "conversations with yourself" referred to in Ms. Stoiber's letter to Dr. Brown. Thus, conversations between VA and IOM staff determined the outcome of the report before the IOM committee to prepare the report was ever appointed.

In summary, VA and the IOM have not complied with the law requiring the IOM Gulf War reports, restricting the scientific evidence required to be considered. This action has been deliberate. Conversations between VA and IOM staff have shaped the methodology of the reports so as to predetermine their outcome. Dr. Brown and Ms. Stoiber are long gone, and their successors are more careful regarding what they put in writing, but the corrupted Categories of Asssociation and all the IOM reports based on them still stand.

4. The IOM has recently applied this same corrupt standard to the health of recent Iraq and Afghanistan veterans, denying the adverse effects of toxic substances released by burn pits.

In 2007 on-site military officers with environmental health responsibilities reported dangerous health effects of toxic exposures from burn pits on U.S. bases in Iraq and Afghanistan, particularly Joint Base Balad (JBB). A draft executive summary of a study, dated December 2007, showed dioxin levels at 51 times acceptable levels, particulate exposure at 50 times acceptable levels, volatile compounds at two times acceptable levels, and cancer risk from exposure to dioxins at two times acceptable levels for people at Balad for a year and at eight times acceptable levels for people at the base for more than a year.

DoD Washington said the draft summary contained "incorrect data" due to a "software error" and was "prematurely distributed." Officials in Washington in the DoD Office of Force Health Protection and Readiness denied any lasting health effects: "While exposure to burn pit smoke may cause temporary coughing and redness or stinging of the eyes, extensive environmental monitoring indicates that smoke exposures not interfering with breathing or requiring medical treatment at the time of exposure usually do not cause any lasting health effects or medical follow-up." http://www.armytimes.com/article/20081027/NEWS/810270315/Burn-pit-at-Balad-raises-health-concerns

An IOM report was ordered by VA to study the subject. "[T]he Institute of Medicine has embarked on a comprehensive study with noted experts in environmental and occupational health to study the issue." "Is Burn Pit Smoke Hazardous To Your Health?", Force Health Protection and Readiness magazine, vol. 5, issue 2, 2010, page 11.

http://home.fhpr.osd.mil/Libraries/FHPR—Online—Magazine/Volume—5—Issue—2.sflb.ashx

Following the pattern established in the IOM Gulf War reports, the IOM burn pit report first pointed out the known health risks of the exposures: "Chemicals in all three major classes of chemicals detected at JBB . . . have been associated with long-term health effects. A wide array of health effects have been observed in humans and animals after exposure to the specific pollutants detected at JBB . . . The health-effects data on the other pollutants detected include: neurological effects, liver toxicity and reduced liver function, cancer, respiratory toxicity and morbidity, kidney toxicity and reduced kidney function, blook effects, cardiovascular toxicity and morbidity, reproductive and developmental toxicity." http://books.nap.edu/openbook.php?record—id=13209&page=5

But then, when it came to arriving at conclusions, the IOM committee applied the Categories of Association that allowed only for consideration of human studies. It stated that it was "[f]ollowing the methods and criteria used by other IOM committees that have prepared reports for the Gulf War and Health Series and the Veterans and Agent Orange Series . . .") http://books.nap.edu/openbook.php?record—id=13209&page=6).

There were no published studies of service members exposed to burn pits, so the committee relied on studies of groups like firefighters and incinerator workers. Accordingly, as reported on VA's website, the committee found only "limited but suggestive evidence of a link between exposure to combustion products and reduced lung function" and "inadequate or insufficient evidence of a relation to combustion products and cancer, respiratory diseases, circulatory diseases, neurological diseases, and adverse reproductive and developmental outcomes." It did not find the "sufficient evidence of an association" required for service connection.

http://www.publichealth.va.gov/exposures/burnpits/health-effects-studies.asp

Thus, rigging IOM reports by corrupting the Categories of Association has been extended to a new generation of veterans, as well as continuing for Gulf War veterans.

ATTACHMENTS TO APPENDIX A

TITLE 38—VETERANS' BENEFITS,

PART II—GENERAL BENEFITS

CHAPTER 11—COMPENSATION FOR SERVICE–CONNECTED DISABILITY OR DEATH, SUBCHAPTER II—WARTIME DISABILITY COMPENSATION

Sec. 1117. Compensation for disabilities occurring in Persian Gulf War veterans

* * *

Agreement With National Academy of Sciences Regarding Toxic Drugs and Illnesses Associated With Gulf War

Pub. L. 105–277, div. C, title XVI, Sec. 1603–1605, Oct. 21, 1998, 112 Stat. 2681–745 to 2681–748, as amended by Pub. L. 107–103, title II, Sec. 202(d)(2), Dec. 27, 2001, 115 Stat. 989, provided that:

"SEC. 1603. AGREEMENT WITH NATIONAL ACADEMY OF SCIENCES.

"(a) Purpose.—The purpose of this section is to provide for the National Academy of Sciences, an independent nonprofit scientific organization with appropriate expertise, to review and evaluate the available scientific evidence regarding associations between illnesses and exposure to toxic agents, environmental or wartime hazards, or preventive medicines or vaccines associated with Gulf War service.

"(b) Agreement.—The Secretary of Veterans Affairs shall seek to enter into an agreement with the National Academy of Sciences for the Academy to perform the activities covered by this section. The Secretary shall seek to enter into the agreement not later than two months after the date of enactment of this Act [Oct. 21, 1998].

"(c) Identification of Agents and Illnesses.—(1) Under the agreement under subsection (b), the National Academy of Sciences shall——

"(A) identify the biological, chemical, or other toxic agents, environmental or wartime hazards, or preventive medicines or vaccines to which members of the Armed Forces who served in the Southwest Asia theater of operations during the Persian Gulf War may have been exposed by reason of such service; and

"(B) identify the illnesses (including diagnosed illnesses and undiagnosed illnesses) that are manifest in such members.

"(2) In identifying illnesses under paragraph (1)(B), the Academy shall review and summarize the relevant scientific evidence regarding illnesses among the members described in paragraph (1)(A) and among other appropriate populations of individuals, including mortality, symptoms, and adverse reproductive health outcomes among such members and individuals.

"(d) Initial Consideration of Specific Agents.—(1) In identifying under subsection (c) the agents, hazards, or preventive medicines or vaccines to which members of the Armed Forces may have been exposed for purposes of the first report under subsection (i), the National Academy of Sciences shall consider, within the first six months after the date of enactment of this Act [Oct. 21, 1998], the following:

"(A) The following organophosphorous pesticides:

"(i) Chlorpyrifos.

"(ii) Diazinon.

"(iii) Dichlorvos.

"(iv) Malathion.

"(B) The following carbamate pesticides:

"(i) Proxpur.

"(ii) Carbaryl.

"(iii) Methomyl.

"(C) The carbamate pyridostigmine bromide used as nerve agent prophylaxis.

"(D) The following chlorinated hydrocarbon and other pesticides and repellents:

"(i) Lindane.

"(ii) Pyrethrins.

"(iii) Permethrins.

"(iv) Rodenticides (bait).

"(v) Repellent (DEET).

"(E) The following low-level nerve agents and precursor compounds at exposure levels below those which produce immediately apparent incapacitating symptoms:

"(i) Sarin.

"(ii) Tabun.

"(F) The following synthetic chemical compounds:

"(i) Mustard agents at levels below those which cause immediate blistering.

"(ii) Volatile organic compounds.

"(iii) Hydrazine.

"(iv) Red fuming nitric acid.

"(v) Solvents.

"(vi) Uranium.

"(G) The following ionizing radiation:

"(i) Depleted uranium.

"(ii) Microwave radiation.

"(iii) Radio frequency radiation.

"(H) The following environmental particulates and pollutants:

"(i) Hydrogen sulfide.

"(ii) Oil fire byproducts.

"(iii) Diesel heater fumes.

"(iv) Sand micro-particles.

"(I) Diseases endemic to the region (including the following):

"(i) Leishmaniasis.

"(ii) Sandfly fever.

"(iii) Pathogenic escherechia coli.

"(iv) Shigellosis.

"(J) Time compressed administration of multiple live, 'attenuated', and toxoid vaccines.

"(2) The consideration of agents, hazards, and medicines and vaccines under paragraph (1) shall not preclude the Academy from identifying other agents, hazards, or medicines or vaccines to which members of the Armed Forces may have been exposed for purposes of any report under subsection (i).

"(3) Not later than six months after the date of enactment of this Act [Oct. 21, 1998], the Academy shall submit to the designated congressional committees a report specifying the agents, hazards, and medicines and vaccines considered under paragraph (1).

"(e) Determinations of Associations Between Agents and Illnesses.——

(1) For each agent, hazard, or medicine or vaccine and illness identified under subsection (c), the National Academy of Sciences shall determine, to the extent that available scientific data permit meaningful determinations——

"(A) whether a statistical association exists between exposure to the agent, hazard, or medicine or vaccine and the illness, taking into account the strength of the scientific evidence and the appropriateness of the scientific methodology used to detect the association;

"(B) the increased risk of the illness among human or animal populations exposed to the agent, hazard, or medicine or vaccine; and

"(C) whether a plausible biological mechanism or other evidence of a causal relationship exists between exposure to the agent, hazard, or medicine or vaccine and the illness.

"(2) The Academy shall include in its reports under subsection (i) a full discussion of the scientific evidence and reasoning that led to its conclusions under this subsection.

"(f) Review of Potential Treatment Models for Certain Illnesses.——Under the agreement under subsection (b), the National Academy of Sciences shall separately review, for each chronic undiagnosed illness identified under subsection (c)(1)(B) and for any other chronic illness that the Academy determines to warrant such review, the available scientific data in order to identify empirically valid models of treatment for such illnesses which employ successful treatment modalities for populations with similar symptoms.

"(g) Recommendations for Additional Scientific Studies.—(1) Under the agreement under subsection (b), the National Academy of Sciences shall make any recommendations that it considers appropriate for additional scientific studies (including studies relating to treatment models) to resolve areas of continuing scientific uncertainty relating to the health consequences of exposure to toxic agents, environmental or wartime hazards, or preventive medicines or vaccines associated with Gulf War service.

"(2) In making recommendations for additional studies, the Academy shall consider the available scientific data, the value and relevance of the information that could result from such studies, and the cost and feasibility of carrying out such studies.

"(h) Subsequent Reviews.—(1) Under the agreement under subsection (b), the National Academy of Sciences shall conduct on a periodic and ongoing basis additional reviews of the evidence and data relating to its activities under this section.

"(2) As part of each review under this subsection, the Academy shall——

"(A) conduct as comprehensive a review as is practicable of the evidence referred to in subsection (c) and the data referred to in subsections (e), (f), and (g) that became available since the last review of such evidence and data under this section; and

"(B) make determinations under the subsections referred to in subparagraph (A) on the basis of the results of such review and all other reviews previously conducted for purposes of this section.

"(i) Reports.—(1) Under the agreement under subsection (b), the National Academy of Sciences shall submit to the committees and officials referred to in paragraph (5) periodic written reports regarding the Academy's activities under the agreement.

"(2) The first report under paragraph (1) shall be submitted not later than 18 months after the date of enactment of this Act [Oct. 21, 1998]. That report shall include——

"(A) the determinations and discussion referred to in subsection (e);

"(B) the results of the review of models of treatment under subsection (f); and

"(C) any recommendations of the Academy under subsection (g).

"(3) Reports shall be submitted under this subsection at least once every two years, as measured from the date of the report under paragraph (2).

"(4) In any report under this subsection (other than the report under paragraph (2)), the Academy may specify an absence of meaningful developments in the scientific or medical community with respect to the activities of the Academy under this section during the 2-year period ending on the date of such report.

"(5) Reports under this subsection shall be submitted to the following:

"(A) The designated congressional committees.

"(B) The Secretary of Veterans Affairs.

"(C) The Secretary of Defense.

"(j) Sunset.—This section shall cease to be effective on October 1, 2010.

"(k) Alternative Contract Scientific Organization.—(1) If the Secretary is unable within the time period set forth in subsection (b) to enter into an agreement with the National Academy of Sciences for the purposes of this section on terms acceptable to the Secretary, the Secretary shall seek to enter into an agreement for purposes of this section with another appropriate scientific organization that is not part of the Government, operates as a not-for-profit entity, and has expertise and objectivity comparable to that of the National Academy of Sciences.

"(2) If the Secretary enters into an agreement with another organization under this subsection, any reference in this section and section 1118 of title 38, United States Code (as added by section 1602(a)), to the National Academy of Sciences shall be treated as a reference to such other organization.

"SEC. 1604. REPEAL OF INCONSISTENT PROVISIONS OF LAW.

"In the event of the enactment, before, on, or after the date of the enactment of this Act [Oct. 21, 1998], of section 101 of the Veterans Programs Enhancement Act of 1998 [Pub. L. 105–368, 112 Stat. 3317], or any similar provision of law enacted during the second session of the 105th Congress requiring an agreement with the National Academy of Sciences regarding an evaluation of health consequences of service in Southwest Asia during the Persian Gulf War, such section 101 (or other provision of law) shall be treated as if never enacted, and shall have no force or effect.

"SEC. 1605. DEFINITIONS.

"In this title [enacting section 1118 of this title, amending this section and section 1113 of this title, and enacting this note and provisions set out as a note under section 101 of this title]:

"(1) The term 'toxic agent, environmental or wartime hazard, or preventive medicine or vaccine associated with Gulf War service' means a biological, chemical, or other toxic agent, environmental or wartime hazard, or preventive medicine or vaccine that is known or presumed to be associated with service in the Armed Forces in the Southwest Asia theater of operations during the Persian Gulf War, whether such association arises as a result of single, repeated, or sustained exposure and whether such association arises through exposure singularly or in combination.

"(2) The term 'designated congressional committees' means the following:

"(A) The Committees on Veterans' Affairs and Armed Services of the Senate.

"(B) The Committees on Veterans' Affairs and National Security [now Armed Services] of the House of Representatives.

"(3) The term 'Persian Gulf War' has the meaning given that term in section 101(33) of title 38, United States Code."

[Pub. L. 105–368, title I, Sec. 101, Nov. 11, 1998, 112 Stat. 3317, enacted provisions similar to those in sections 1603 and 1605 of Pub. L. 105–277, set out above. See section 1604 of Pub. L. 105–277, set out above.]

From the U.S. Code Online via GPO Access
[www.gpoaccess.gov]
[Laws in effect as of January 3, 2007]
[CITE: 38USC1118]

TITLE 38—VETERANS' BENEFITS

PART II—GENERAL BENEFITS

CHAPTER 11—COMPENSATION FOR SERVICE–CONNECTED DISABILITY OR DEATH

SUBCHAPTER II—WARTIME DISABILITY COMPENSATION

Sec. 1118. Presumptions of service connection for illnesses associated with service in the Persian Gulf during the Persian Gulf War

(a)(1) For purposes of section 1110 of this title, and subject to section 1113 of this title, each illness, if any, described in paragraph (2) shall be considered to have been incurred in or aggravated by service referred to in that paragraph, notwithstanding that there is no record of evidence of such illness during the period of such service.

(2) An illness referred to in paragraph (1) is any diagnosed or undiagnosed illness that——

(A) the Secretary determines in regulations prescribed under this section to warrant a presumption of service connection by reason of having a positive association with exposure to a biological, chemical, or other toxic agent, environmental or wartime hazard, or preventive medicine or vaccine known or presumed to be associated with service in the Armed Forces in the Southwest Asia theater of operations during the Persian Gulf War; and

(B) becomes manifest within the period, if any, prescribed in such regulations in a veteran who served on active duty in that theater of operations during that war and by reason of such service was exposed to such agent, hazard, or medicine or vaccine.

(3) For purposes of this subsection, a veteran who served on active duty in the Southwest Asia theater of operations during the Persian Gulf War and has an illness described in paragraph (2) shall be presumed to have been exposed by reason

of such service to the agent, hazard, or medicine or vaccine associated with the illness in the regulations prescribed under this section unless there is conclusive evidence to establish that the veteran was not exposed to the agent, hazard, or medicine or vaccine by reason of such service.

(4) For purposes of this section, signs or symptoms that may be a manifestation of an undiagnosed illness include the signs and symptoms listed in section 1117(g) of this title.

(b)(1)(A) Whenever the Secretary makes a determination described in subparagraph (B), the Secretary shall prescribe regulations providing that a presumption of service connection is warranted for the illness covered by that determination for purposes of this section.

(B) A determination referred to in subparagraph (A) is a determination based on sound medical and scientific evidence that a positive association exists between——

(i) the exposure of humans or animals to a biological, chemical, or other toxic agent, environmental or wartime hazard, or preventive medicine or vaccine known or presumed to be associated with service in the Southwest Asia theater of operations during the Persian Gulf War; and

(ii) the occurrence of a diagnosed or undiagnosed illness in humans or animals.

(2)(A) In making determinations for purposes of paragraph (1), the Secretary shall take into account——

(i) the reports submitted to the Secretary by the National Academy of Sciences under section 1603 of the Persian Gulf War Veterans Act of 1998; and

(ii) all other sound medical and scientific information and analyses available to the Secretary.

(B) In evaluating any report, information, or analysis for purposes of making such determinations, the Secretary shall take into consideration whether the results are statistically significant, are capable of replication, and withstand peer review.

(3) An association between the occurrence of an illness in humans or animals and exposure to an agent, hazard, or medicine or vaccine shall be considered to be positive for purposes of this subsection if the credible evidence for the association is equal to or outweighs the credible evidence against the association.

(c)(1) Not later than 60 days after the date on which the Secretary receives a report from the National Academy of Sciences under section 1603 of the Persian Gulf War Veterans Act of 1998, the Secretary shall determine whether or not a presumption of service connection is warranted for each illness, if any, covered by the report.

(2) If the Secretary determines under this subsection that a presumption of service connection is warranted, the Secretary shall, not later than 60 days after making the determination, issue proposed regulations setting forth the Secretary's determination.

(3)(A) If the Secretary determines under this subsection that a presumption of service connection is not warranted, the Secretary shall, not later than 60 days after making the determination, publish in the Federal Register a notice of the determination. The notice shall include an explanation of the scientific basis for the determination.

(B) If an illness already presumed to be service connected under this section is subject to a determination under subparagraph (A), the Secretary shall, not later than 60 days after publication of the notice under that subparagraph, issue proposed regulations removing the presumption of service connection for the illness.

(4) Not later than 90 days after the date on which the Secretary issues any proposed regulations under this subsection, the Secretary shall issue final regulations. Such regulations shall be effective on the date of issuance.

(d) Whenever the presumption of service connection for an illness under this section is removed under subsection (c)——

(1) a veteran who was awarded compensation for the illness on the basis of the presumption before the effective date of the removal of the presumption shall continue to be entitled to receive compensation on that basis; and

(2) a survivor of a veteran who was awarded dependency and indemnity compensation for the death of a veteran resulting from the illness on the basis of the presumption before that date shall continue to be entitled to receive dependency and indemnity compensation on that basis.

(e) Subsections (b) through (d) shall cease to be effective on September 30, 2011.

(Added Pub. L. 105–277, div. C, title XVI, Sec. 1602(a)(1), Oct. 21, 1998, 112 Stat. 2681–742; amended Pub. L. 107–103, title II, Sec. 202(b)(2), (d)(1), Dec. 27, 2001, 115 Stat. 989.)

References in Text

Section 1603 of the Persian Gulf War Veterans Act of 1998, referred to in subsecs. (b)(2)(A)(i) and (c)(1), is section 1603 of Pub. L. 105-277, which is set out in a note under section 1117 of this title.

Amendments

2001—Subsec. (a)(4). Pub. L. 107–103, Sec. 202(b)(2), added par. (4).

Subsec. (e). Pub. L. 107–103, Sec. 202(d)(1), substituted "on September 30, 2011" for "10 years after the first day of the fiscal year in which the National Academy of Sciences submits to the Secretary the first report under section 1603 of the Persian Gulf War Veterans Act of 1998".

Effective Date of 2001 Amendment

Amendment by section 202(b)(2) of Pub. L. 107–103 effective Mar. 1, 2002, see section 202(c) of Pub. L. 107–103, set out as a note under section 1117 of this title.

Gulf War and Health, Vol. 1, p. 72 [emphasis added]

studies often focus on one agent at a time, they more easily enable the study of chemical mixtures and their potential interactions.

Research on health effects of toxic substance includes animal studies that characterize absorption, distribution, metabolism, elimination, and excretion. Animal studies may examine acute (short-term) exposures or chronic (long-term) exposures. Animal research may focus on the mechanism of action (i.e., how the toxin exerts its deleterious effects at the cellular and molecular levels). Mechanism-of-action (or mechanistic) studies encompass a range of laboratory approaches with whole animals and in vitro systems using tissues or cells from humans or animals. Also, structure-activity relationships, in which comparisons are made between the molecular structure and chemical and physical properties of a potential toxin versus a known toxin, are an important source of hypotheses about mechanism of action.

In carrying out its charge, the committee used animal and other nonhuman studies in several ways, particularly as a marker for health effects that might be important for humans. If an agent, for example, was absorbed and deposited in specific tissues or organs (e.g., uranium deposition in bone and kidney), the committee looked especially closely for possible abnormalities at these sites in human studies.

One of the problems with animal studies, however, is the difficulty of finding animal models to study symptoms that relate to uniquely human attributes, such as cognition, purposive behavior, and the perception of pain. With the exception of fatigue, many symptoms reported by veterans (e.g., headache, muscle or joint pain) are difficult to study in standard neurotoxicological tests in animals (OTA, 1990).

For its evaluation and categorization of the degree of association between each exposure and a human health effect, however, the committee only used evidence from human studies. Nevertheless, the committee did use nonhuman studies as the basis for judgments about biologic plausibility, which is one of the criteria for establishing causation (see below).

HUMAN STUDIES

EPIDEMIOLOGIC STUDIES

Epidemiology concerns itself with the relationship of various factors and conditions that determine the frequency and distribution of an infectious process, a disease, or a physiological state in human populations (Lilienfeld, 1978). Its focus on populations distinguishes it from other medical disciplines. Epidemiologic studies characterize the relationship between the agent, the environment, and the host and are useful for generating and testing hypotheses with respect to the association between exposure to an agent and health or disease. The following section describes the major types of epidemiologic studies considered by the committee.

Gulf War and Health, Vol. 2, p. 13 [emphasis added]

general use in the United States (PAC, 1996) at that time. However, EPA has since placed restrictions on some of the insecticides used during the Gulf War.

USE OF SOLVENTS IN THE GULF WAR

To determine the specific solvents used in the Gulf War the committee gathered information from several sources, including veterans, OSAGWI (2000), and DOD's Defense Logistics Agency. As a result of its research, the committee ultimately identified 53 solvents for review (Appendix D).

There is little information to characterize the use of solvents in the Gulf War. Wartime uses of solvents (such as vehicle maintenance and repair, cleaning, and degreasing) probably paralleled stateside military or civilian uses of solvents, but operating conditions in the Gulf War (such as ventilation and the use of masks) may have varied widely from stateside working conditions.

The most thoroughly documented solvent exposure involved spray-painting with chemical-agent-resistant coating (CARC) (OSAGWI, 2000). Thousands of military vehicles deployed to the Gulf War were painted with tan CARC to provide camouflage protection for the desert environment and a surface that was easily decontaminated. Not all military personnel involved in CARC painting were trained in spray-painting operations, and some might not have had all the necessary personal protective equipment (OSAGWI, 2000).

Personnel engaged in CARC painting were exposed to solvents in the CARC formulations, paint thinners, and cleaning products. As noted in the OSAGWI report, some of the solvents used to clean painting equipment might have been purchased locally and therefore not identified.

COMPLEXITIES IN ADDRESSING GULF WAR HEALTH ISSUES

Investigations of the health effects of past wars often focused on narrowly defined hazards or health outcomes, such as infectious diseases (for example, typhoid and malaria) during the Civil War, specific chemical hazards (for example, mustard gas and Agent Orange) in World War I and Vietnam, and combat injuries. Discussion of the possible health effects of the Gulf War, however, involves many complex issues, such as exposure to multiple agents, lack of exposure information, nonspecific illnesses that lack defined diagnoses or treatment protocols, and the experience of war itself. The committee was not charged with addressing those issues, but it presents them here to acknowledge the difficulties faced by veterans and their families, researchers, policy-makers, and others in trying to understand Gulf War veterans' health.

MULTIPLE EXPOSURES AND CHEMICAL INTERACTIONS

Military personnel were potentially exposed to numerous agents during the Gulf War. The number of agents and the combination of agents to which the veterans may have been exposed make it difficult to determine whether any one agent or combination of agents is the cause of the veterans' illnesses. These include preventive measures (such as use of pyridostigmine bromide, vaccines, and insecticides), hazards of the natural environment

Gulf War and Health, Vol. 1, p. 83 [emphasis added]

mittee evaluated the strength of the evidence for or against associations between health effects and exposure to the agents being studied.

CATEGORIES OF ASSOCIATION

The committee used five previously established categories to classify the evidence for association between exposure to a specific agent and a health outcome. The categories closely resemble those used by several IOM committees that evaluated vaccine safety (IOM, 1991, 1994a), herbicides used in Vietnam (IOM, 1994b, 1996, 1999), and indoor pollutants related to asthma (IOM, 2000). Although the categories imply a statistical association, the committee had sufficient epidemiologic evidence to examine statistical associations for only one of the agents under study (i.e., depleted uranium), there was very limited epidemiologic evidence for the other agents examined (i.e., sarin, pyridostigmine bromide, and anthrax and botulinum toxoid vaccines). Thus, the committee based its conclusions on the strength and coherence of the data in the available studies. In many cases, these data distinguished differences between transient and long-term health outcomes related to the dose of the agent. Based on the literature, it became incumbent on the committee to similarly specify the differences between dose levels and the nature of the health outcomes. This approach led the committee to reach conclusions about long- and short-term health effects, as well as health outcomes related to the dose of the putative agents. The final conclusions expressed in Chapters 4–7 represent the committee's collective judgment. The committee endeavored to express its judgments as clearly and precisely as the available data allowed. The committee used the established categories of association from previous IOM studies, because they have gained wide acceptance for more than a decade by Congress, government agencies, researchers, and veteran groups.

- Sufficient Evidence of a Causal Relationship. Evidence is sufficient to conclude that a causal relationship exists between the exposure to a specific agent and a health outcome in humans. The evidence fulfills the criteria for sufficient evidence of an association (below) and satisfies several of the criteria used to assess causality:

strength of association, dose-response relationship, consistency of association, temporal relationship, specificity of association, and biological plausibility.

- Sufficient Evidence of an Association. Evidence is sufficient to conclude that there is a positive association. That is, a positive association has been observed between an exposure to a specific agent and a health outcome in human studies in which chance, bias, and confounding could be ruled out with reasonable confidence.

- Limited/Suggestive Evidence of an Association. Evidence is suggestive of an association between exposure to a specific agent and a health outcome in humans, but is limited because chance, bias, and confounding could not be ruled out with confidence.

Gulf War and Health, Vol. 1, p. 84 [emphasis added]

- Inadequate/Insufficient Evidence to Determine Whether an Association Does or Does Not Exist. The available studies are of insufficient quality, consistency, or statistical power to permit a conclusion regarding the presence or absence of an association between an exposure to a specific agent and a health outcome in humans.

- Limited/Suggestive Evidence of No Association. There are several adequate studies, covering the full range of levels of exposure that humans are known to encounter, that are mutually consistent in not showing a positive association between exposure to a specific agent and a health outcome at any level of exposure. A conclusion of no association is inevitably limited to the conditions, levels of exposure, and length of observation covered by the available studies. In addition, the possibility of a very small elevation in risk at the levels of exposure studied can never be excluded.

These five categories cover different degrees or levels of association, with the highest level being sufficient evidence of a causal relationship between exposure to a specific agent and a health outcome. The criteria for each category incorporate key points discussed earlier in this chapter. A recurring theme is that an association is more likely to be valid if it is possible to reduce or eliminate common sources of error in making inferences: chance, bias, and confounding. Accordingly, the criteria for each category express varying degrees of confidence based upon the extent to which it has been possible to exclude these sources of error. To infer a causal relationship from a body of evidence, the committee relied on long-standing criteria for assessing causation in epidemiology (Hill, 1971; Evans, 1976).

COMMENTS ON INCREASED RISK OF ADVERSE HEALTH OUTCOMES AMONG GULF WAR VETERANS

As discussed in the beginning of this chapter, the committee reviewed the available scientific evidence in the peer-reviewed literature in order to draw conclusions about associations between the agents of interest and adverse health effects in all populations. The committee placed its conclusions in categories that reflect the strength of the evidence for an association between exposure to the agent and health outcomes. The committee could not measure the likelihood that Gulf War veterans' health problems are associated with or caused by these agents. To address this issue, the committee would need to compare the rates of health effects in Gulf War veterans exposed to the putative agents with the rates of those who were not exposed, which would require information about the agents to which individual veterans were exposed and their doses. However, as discussed throughout this report, there is a paucity of data regarding the actual agents and doses to which individual Gulf War veterans were exposed. Further, to answer questions about increased risk of illnesses in Gulf War veterans, it would also be important to know the degree to which any other differences be-

Veterans and Agent Orange: Update 1996, p. 97 [emphasis added]

Summary Of The Evidence

Categories of Association

The categories of association used by the committee were those used in VAO. Consistent with the charge to the Secretary of Veterans Affairs in P.L. 102–4, the distinctions between the categories are based on "statistical association," not on causality. Thus, standard criteria used in epidemiology for assessing causality (Hill, 1971) do not strictly apply. The distinctions between the categories reflect the committee's judgment that a statistical association would be found in a large, well-designed epidemiologic study of the outcome in question in which exposure to herbicides or dioxin was sufficiently high, well-characterized, and appropriately measured. The categories of association are:

- Sufficient Evidence of an Association Evidence is sufficient to conclude that there is a positive association. That is, a positive association has been observed between herbicides and the outcome in studies in which chance, bias, and confounding could be ruled out with reasonable confidence. For example, if several small studies that are free from bias and confounding show an association that is consistent in magnitude and direction, there may be sufficient evidence for an association.

- Limited/Suggestive Evidence of an Association Evidence is suggestive of an association between herbicides and the outcome but is limited because chance, bias, and confounding could not be ruled out with confidence. For example, at least one high-quality study shows a positive association but the results of other studies are inconsistent.

- Inadequate/Insufficient Evidence to Determine Whether an Association Exists The available studies are of insufficient quality, consistency, or statistical power to permit a conclusion regarding the presence or absence of an association. For example, studies fail to control for confounding, have inadequate exposure assessment, or fail to address latency.

- Limited/Suggestive Evidence of No Association There are several adequate studies, cover the full range of levels of exposure that human beings are known to encounter, that are mutually consistent in not showing a positive association between exposure to herbicides and the outcome at any level of exposure. A conclusion of "no association" is inevitably limited to the conditions, level of exposure, and length of observation covered by the available studies. In addition, the possibility of a very small elevation in risk at the levels of exposure studied can never be excluded.

Gulf War and Health, Vol. 1, p. 72 [emphasis added]

studies often focus on one agent at a time, they more easily enable the study of chemical mixtures and their potential interactions.

Research on health effects of toxic substance includes animal studies that characterize absorption, distribution, metabolism, elimination, and excretion. Animal studies may examine acute (short-term) exposures or chronic (long-term) exposures. Animal research may focus on the mechanism of action (i.e., how the toxin exerts its deleterious effects at the cellular and molecular levels). Mechanism-of-action (or mechanistic) studies encompass a range of laboratory approaches with whole animals and in vitro systems using tissues or cells from humans or animals. Also, structure-activity relationships, in which comparisons are made between the molecular structure and chemical and physical properties of a potential toxin versus a known toxin, are an important source of hypotheses about mechanism of action.

In carrying out its charge, the committee used animal and other nonhuman studies in several ways, particularly as a marker for health effects that might be important for humans. If an agent, for example, was absorbed and deposited in specific tissues or organs (e.g., uranium deposition in bone and kidney), the committee looked especially closely for possible abnormalities at these sites in human studies.

One of the problems with animal studies, however, is the difficulty of finding animal models to study symptoms that relate to uniquely human attributes, such as cognition, purposive behavior, and the perception of pain. With the exception of fatigue, many symptoms reported by veterans (e.g., headache, muscle or joint pain) are difficult to study in standard neurotoxicological tests in animals (OTA, 1990).

For its evaluation and categorization of the degree of association between each exposure and a human health effect, however, the committee only used evidence from human studies. Nevertheless, the committee did use nonhuman studies as the basis for judgments about biologic plausibility, which is one of the criteria for establishing causation (see below).

HUMAN STUDIES

EPIDEMIOLOGIC STUDIES

Epidemiology concerns itself with the relationship of various factors and conditions that determine the frequency and distribution of an infectious process, a disease, or a physiological state in human populations (Lilienfeld, 1978). Its focus on populations distinguishes it from other medical disciplines. Epidemiologic studies characterize the relationship between the agent, the environment, and the host and are useful for generating and testing hypotheses with respect to the association between exposure to an agent and health or disease. The following section describes the major types of epidemiologic studies considered by the committee.

THE SECRETARY OF VETERANS AFFAIRS

WASHINGTON

January 24, 2003

Harvey Fineberg, M.D., Ph.D.
President
Institute of Medicine
The National Academies
500 Fifth Street, NW
Washington, DC 20001

Dear Dr. Fineberg:

The Department of Veterans Affairs appreciates and respects the excellent work contained in the Institute of Medicine (IOM) report on "Gulf War Health." As you know, this report was completed in 2000 in response to a Congressional requirement. The IOM, at that time, reviewed medical and scientific literature on the health effects of certain materials, including Sarin, that Gulf War veterans may have been exposed to during the 1991 Gulf War.

Recently, a number of new studies have been published on the effects of Sarin on laboratory animals. These studies have raised concerns with Gulf War veterans and other Americans regarding the relationship of these studies to possible health consequences of human exposures.

With this in mind, I am requesting IOM examine the medical and scientific literature on health effects of Sarin published since the 2000 Report. I ask that IOM report back to VA, as soon as possible, on whether this new research affects earlier conclusions of IOM. Specifically, in the interest of veterans' health, we would like to know if this new scientific information alters the conclusions about possible long-term health consequences of exposure to low levels of Sarin.

We look forward to meeting with you to discuss additional specifics and timing for this report. If you have any questions about this request, please contact Dr. Susan Mather, Chief Officer, Office of Public Health and Environmental Hazards, at (202) 273-8575.

Sincerely yours,

Anthony J. Principi

Updated Literature Review of Sarin (2004), p. 20 [emphasis added]

OP insecticide data in its conclusion, the committee reviewed the OP epidemiology literature. The committee responsible for GW2 (IOM, 2003a) reviewed the literature on OP compounds. The present committee reviewed relevant epidemiology studies published since the preparation of that report.

Animal studies had a small role in the committee's assessment of association between putative agents and health outcomes. As with previous committees, this committee used animal data for making assessments of biologic plausibility in support of the epidemiologic data rather than as part of the weight of evidence to determine the likelihood that an exposure to a specific agent might cause a long-term outcome.

The committee classified the evidence of an association between exposure to sarin and cyclosarin and a specific health outcome into five categories (Box 1–1). The categories closely resemble those used by previous committees that evaluated the effects of chemicals related to the Gulf War (IOM, 2000a, 2003a) and those used by several IOM committees that have evaluated vaccine safety (IOM, 1991, 1994a), herbicides used in Vietnam (IOM, 1994b, 1996, 1999, 2001, 2003b), and indoor pollutants related to asthma (IOM, 2000b). The committee's conclusions, presented in Chapter 4, represent its collective judgment.

The committee endeavored to express its judgment as clearly and precisely as the available data allowed, and it used the established categories of association from previous IOM studies because they have gained wide acceptance over more

BOX 1–1fi CATEGORIES OF EVIDENCE

Sufficient Evidence of a Causal Relationship

Evidence from available studies is sufficient to conclude that a causal relationship exists between exposure to a specific agent and a specific health outcome in humans, and the evidence is supported by experimental data. The evidence fulfills the guidelines for sufficient evidence of an association (below) and satisfies several of the guidelines used to assess causality: strength of association, dose-response relationship, consistency of association, biologic plausibility, and a temporal relationship.

Sufficient Evidence of an Association

Evidence from available studies is sufficient to conclude that there is a positive association. A consistent positive association has been observed between exposure to a specific agent and a specific health outcome in human studies in which chance1 and bias, including confounding, could be ruled out with reasonable confidence. For example, several high-quality studies report consistent positive associations, and the studies are sufficiently free of bias, including adequate control for confounding.

INSTITUTE OF MEDICINE
OF THE NATIONAL ACADEMIES

Susanne A. Stoiber
Executive Director

March 11, 2003

RE: NAS Proposal No. 03-IOM-051-01

Mark A. Brown, Ph.D.
Director
Environmental Agents Service (131)
Department of Veterans Affairs
810 Vermont Avenue, N.W.
Washington, DC 20420

Dear Dr. Brown:

We are pleased to submit the enclosed proposal, prepared by our Board on Health Promotion and Disease Prevention, in response to the Department of Veterans Affairs' (VA) request for an additional deliverable, Gulf War and Health: Updated Review of the Literature on Sarin, under Task Order #VA-2794-123. The total estimated cost of this project is $100,000.00 for the period from April 1, 2003 to October 31, 2003. As discussed with Institute of Medicine staff, there are sufficient funds remaining in the Gulf War and Health, Volume 2 budget to support this task. A no-cost extension has been requested to allow time to complete this task.

This proposal follows a request from Secretary Anthony J. Principi and discussions with yourself requesting an update of the health effects of the chemical warfare agent sarin; the original review of the health effects of sarin was part of Gulf War and Health, Volume 1. The request comes following the publication of new toxicology studies (three) showing effects in rats following exposure to chronic low doses of sarin and subsequent questions from veterans on whether those results would alter the conclusions of Gulf War and Health, Volume 1.

Commencement of this activity is subject to approval by the Executive Committee of the National Research Council Governing Board at its meeting on March 18, 2003.

Mark A. Brown, Ph.D
March 11, 2003
Page 2

The responsible staff officer for this study is Michelle Catlin, Ph.D., Senior Program Officer, 202-334-2777. She may be contacted regarding program matters. Business negotiations are the responsibility of Linda Kilroy, Contract Manager, Office of Contracts and Grants. She may be reached at 202-334-2428.

We shall appreciate your consideration of this matter.

Sincerely,

Susanne A. Stoiber

cc: Secretary Anthony J. Principi

Enclosures

THE NATIONAL ACADEMIES

INSTITUTE OF MEDICINE
Board on Health Promotion and Disease Prevention

SUMMARY

The purpose of this project is to comprehensively review, evaluate, and summarize the available scientific and medical information, published since *Gulf War and Health: Volume 1 Depleted Uranium, Pyridostigmine Bromide, Sarin, Vaccines* (IOM, 2000) and *Gulf War and Health: Volume 2 Insecticides and Solvents* (IOM, 2003), regarding the association between sarin and adverse health effects. If published peer-reviewed information is available in Gulf War veteran population, then the potential health risks posed to Gulf War veterans may be considered. Other relevant issues as indicated by literature, such as health effects associated with combinations of chemicals and genetic susceptibilities may also be reviewed.

BACKGROUND

Almost 700,000 US troops participated in the Gulf War. Most troops returned home and resumed their normal activities. However, within a relatively short time, a number of those who had been deployed to the Persian Gulf began to report health problems they believed to be connected to their deployment. Concern was expressed that their health problems might be related to the biologic and chemical compounds to which the troops may have been exposed.

A number of efforts have attempted to address the many issues surrounding the health consequences of deployment to the Persian Gulf. Most notably, the Presidential Advisory Committee on Gulf War Veterans' Illnesses (PAC) was established by President Clinton in May 1995. The PAC's final report recommended that the Department of Veterans Affairs (VA) enter into an agreement with the National Academy of Sciences to "conduct periodic reviews and analyses of the available scientific evidence to determine statistical associations between Gulf War service and morbidity and mortality. Subsequently, two public laws (P.L. 105-368 and P.L. 105-277) were passed requiring that the VA enter into a contract with the NAS to conduct literature reviews on the putative agents and to determine possible health outcomes related to those agents. There are 34 specific agents that require review as indicated by the two public laws.

In 1998, the VA entered into a contract with the IOM to begin a series of studies related to gulf war and health. In the first study, an IOM committee examined six of the 34 putative agents, including: sarin, cyclosarin, pyridostigmine bromide, depleted uranium, anthrax vaccine, and botulinum toxoid vaccine. A seperate IOM committee recently completed the examination of insecticides and solvents. The remaining compounds (as listed in the two public laws) will be reviewed in future studies. In the interim, the VA has recently requested, in response to veterans' concerns, that an updated examination of sarin be conducted. This proposal is for the sarin update only.

PLAN OF ACTION

Statement of Task

The committee will conduct a review of the peer-reviewed literature published since earlier IOM reports on health effects associated with exposure to sarin and related compounds. Relevant epidemiologic studies will be considered. With regard to the toxicologic literature, the committee will generally use review articles to present a broad overview of the toxicology of sarin and to make assessments of biologic plausibility regarding the compound of study and health effects; individual toxicology research papers will be evaluated as warranted.

The committee will make determinations on the strength of the evidence for associations between sarin and human health effects. If published peer-reviewed information is available on the dose of sarin exposure in Gulf War veterans, the committee may address the potential health risks posed to the veterans. The committee may also consider other relevant issues (e.g., exposure to multiple chemical exposure and genetic susceptibilities). The review will include recommendations for additional scientific studies to resolve areas of continued scientific uncertainty when appropriate.

Work Plan

The study will be conducted over a period of 7 months. The committee will conduct its meetings and deliberations via conference calls and email. One short report will be issued.

Expert Committee and Staff

The overall process will be governed by a committee of approximately 6 experts drawn from a broad range of backgrounds, such as toxicology, epidemiology and biostatistics, environmental and occupational health, exposure assessment, and clinical medicine. The committee will have a full staff (study director, senior program officer, research assistant, project assistant). The staff will review the published studies on the compounds of interest and identify key papers for the committee's consideration. The IOM's Board on Health Promotion and Disease Prevention will oversee the project.

Estimated Expenditures

The estimated cost of this project is $100,000 for the period April 1, 2003 to October 31, 2003. There are adequate funds remaining from *Gulf War and Health: Pesticides and Solvents* project to conduct this study; no additional funding from the Department of Veterans Affairs is being requested. A no-cost extension until October 31, 2003 has been requested to allow time for this new study to be completed.

Product and Dissemination Plan

Based upon committee deliberations, a short report will be produced and will be reviewed according to standard National Research Council (NRC) policies and procedures. The report will be distributed to the sponsor and to other interested parties, such as academic researchers, veterans' organizations, and Congress in accordance with the policies of the National Academy of Sciences. Committee members will travel to Washington to conduct briefings as necessary. Copies of the summary will be produced for broader distribution, and made available on the Internet through the National Academy Press (www.nap.edu).

FEDERAL ADVISORY COMMITTEE ACT (FACA)

The Academy has developed interim policies and procedures to implement Section 15 of the Federal Advisory Committee Act, 5, U.S.C. App. sec. 15. Section 15 includes certain requirements regarding public access and conflicts of interest that are applicable to agreements under which the Academy, using a committee, provides advice or recommendations to a Federal agency. In accordance with Section 15 of FACA, the Academy shall submit to the government sponsor(s) following delivery of each applicable report a certification that the policies and procedures of the Academy that implement Section 15 of FACA have been substantively complied with in the performance of the contract/grant/cooperative agreement with respect to the applicable report.

PUBLIC INFORMATION ABOUT THE PROJECT

In order to afford the public greater knowledge of Academy activities and an opportunity to provide comments on those activities, the Academy may post on its website (http://www.national-academies.org) the following information as appropriate under its procedures: (1) notices of meetings open to the public; (2) brief descriptions of projects; (3) committee appointments, if any (including biographies of committee members); (4) report information; and (5) any other pertinent information.

UNIQUE QUALIFICATIONS OF THE INSTITUTE OF MEDICINE

The IOM is the health policy arm of the National Academy of Sciences, which was created by a Congressional charter signed by President Abraham Lincoln in 1863 as a private honorary society dedicated to the furtherance of science and its use for the general welfare. The IOM was chartered in 1970 to enlist distinguished members of the appropriate professions in the examination of policy matters pertaining to the health of the public. Under the terms of this charter, the IOM is called upon to act as an official, yet independent, advisor to the federal government in matters of science. The IOM also acts at its own initiative to identify and examine significant issues of health care, research, and education to which to direct its attention.

The IOM, like other Academy units, is uniquely situated to provide assessments in areas of science, health care, and public policy. Studies are undertaken by distinguished individuals selected for their expertise and experience in the topic under study. To a degree unmatched elsewhere, the IOM can secure the participation of virtually any expert whom it invites to serve. At any given time, the IOM has some 80 expert groups with over 1,100 members examining a great range of problems. With rare exceptions, members serve without compensation

The IOM's Board on Health Promotion and Disease Prevention, which would oversee the proposed study, is broadly concerned with promoting the health of the public, particularly through population-based interventions. The Board examines and develops strategies for disease prevention, taking into account the multiple factors affecting health—genetic endowment, social and environmental conditions, individual behavior (including tobacco use, alcohol consumption, diet, and exercise) and personal preventive services. The Board also addresses both the science base for such interventions and the public health infrastructure, and the education and supply of health professionals necessary for carrying them out.

Throughout all of its work, the Board puts emphasis on population-based interventions as well as clinical preventive services, and on understanding and mitigating risks to the public's health, including environmental, behavioral, and medical. Some of the crosscutting themes that characterize and guide the Board's work are ethical issues in public health, the application of scientific information in public health policymaking, the evaluation of preventive services and population-based interventions, the efficient allocation of societal resources for prevention, and the development of the science base for health promotion and disease prevention, including behavioral science.

The Board on Health Promotion and Disease Prevention maintains an active research program in veterans' health issues, and in related areas such as environmental and occupational health. Representative studies include the landmark *Veterans and Agent Orange* report, *Update 1996*, *Update 1998*, *Update 2000*, and *Update 2002*, and the health effects of exposure to mustard gas and Lewisite, and several reports regarding the health of Persian Gulf veterans.

Letter to IOM President Regarding Imbalanced Membership of 2016 Report Committee

November 28, 2014

Dr. Victor J. Dzau, M.D.
President
Institute of Medicine
500 Fifth St., NW ?
Washington, DC 20001

Dear Dr. Dzau,

As former members of the VA Research Advisory Committee on Gulf War Veterans Illnesses, we are gravely concerned by the makeup of the committee that IOM staff has chosen for the upcoming review of Gulf War health literature. The membership is grossly imbalanced toward the 1990's government position that Gulf War veterans have no special health problem - just what happens after every war, related to psychiatric issues, and not environmental exposures.

Reviving this discredited fiction will cause veterans' doctors to prescribe inappropriate psychiatric medications, and will misdirect research to find effective treatments down blind alleys - an unconscionable breach of the duty owed to veterans and expected of the Institute of Medicine.

Science has conclusively demonstrated that this government position has no scientific validity. Just four years ago, an IOM committee chaired by Dr. Stephen Hauser, former president of the American Neurological Association, reviewed the scientific literature and concluded that the chronic multisymptom illness suffered by an estimated 250,000 Gulf War veterans (over one-third of the 697,000 who deployed) is a physical illness associated with Gulf War service, a "diagnostic entity" that "cannot be reliably ascribed to any known psychiatric disorder," and that "it is likely that Gulf War illness results from an interplay of genetic and environmental factors." http://books.nap.edu/openbook.php?record—id=12835, pages 262, 210, 204, 109, 261

These conclusions reinforced the similar findings and recommendations of our former committee's 452-page 2008 report. Our committee went further to identify the specific environmental exposures responsible, including pesticides, pyridostigmine bromide pills given to troops as a prophylaxis against nerve gas, and possibly low level nerve gas released by the destruction of Iraqi facilities, oil well fires, and multiple vaccinations. In April 2014, our committee published an update report which concluded that "[s]cientific research published since . 2008 . supports and further substantiates the conclusions of the 2008 report." http://www.va.gov/RAC–GWVI/RACReport2014Final.pdf, page 5

Yet, as the attached analysis shows, fully half the individuals selected for the new committee are predisposed toward the discredited 1990's government position, either because they promoted it themselves, or because they are professionally oriented to view such problems as psychiatric and/or unrelated to environmental exposures. The rest of the committee are neutral figures with a background in other neurological conditions like Alzheimer's disease and traumatic brain injuries. No member of the committee has been actively engaged in Gulf War health research in the past decade.

Given that the committee is charged with producing a consensus report, it is wholly foreseeable that its conclusions will end up between the group predisposed to 1990's fictions and those who are neutral but unfamiliar with the subject. Compared to the 2010 IOM report, it will be a reversal toward the discredited 1990's position.

For three years, VA has been engaged in a surreptitious campaign to revive the 1990's government position. Since no scientific support for the position exists, VA staff has resorted to manipulating Gulf War research and reports. The Research Advisory Committee has documented this manipulation in forty-six pages of findings and recommendations in June 2012 and in a draft section of its April 2014 report which had to be removed because VA eliminated the committee's oversight authority. http://www.va.gov/RAC–GWVI/docs/Committee—Documents/CommitteeDocJune2012.pdf https://veterans.house.gov/sites/republicans.veterans.house.gov/files/Binns%2C%20ExhibitBtestimony.pdf

In September, VA's Director of Epidemiology, Dr. Robert Bossarte, and his staff presented findings of two new VA studies to the Research Advisory Committee. One showed that diagnoses given to Gulf War veterans in VA hospitals over a ten-year period were no different than those given to veterans of the same era who did not deploy. The other, a large survey, showed that rates of PTSD and depression were dramatically higher than previously reported by Gulf War veterans.

To an inexperienced observer, it might seem that the research on Gulf War veterans' health was changing. However, Research Advisory Committee members quickly pointed out that Dr. Bossarte and his staff were not telling the whole story. http://www.va.gov/RAC–GWVI/RAC—Recommendation092314.pdf The diagnoses study presentation failed to mention that VA had no diagnostic code for Gulf War illness or chronic multisymptom illness, that VA doctors at this time were trained to consider the illness as psychosomatic, and that veterans who served during the period of greatest toxic exposures were inexplicably excluded from the study. Similarly, the survey presentation did not disclose that the survey was overweighted with mental health questions to the extent that the Committee had repeatedly recommended against sending it out, http://www.va.gov/RAC–GWVI/docs/ Committee—Documents/CommitteeDocJune2012.pdf, Appendix F, and that the survey's principal investigator had testified to Congress that his superiors lied to then-VA Chief of Staff John Gingrich to induce him to release the survey. https://veterans.house.gov/witness-testimony/dr-steven-s-coughlin The presentation did not mention that people suffering from chronic health problems often become depressed after 23 years, but it is not the cause of their illness.

Dr. Bossarte and his staff will be presenting to the new IOM committee on December 3. Very likely they will be presenting their new research findings. But no one on the IOM committee will know that they are not being told the whole story, because there are no members with the necessary background. Thus, misleading VA studies will be presented to an imbalanced IOM committee, which will include the findings in its new report, and science will be "revised".

The motivation behind VA's manipulation of science is clear: to hold down benefits costs and claims wait times. In April, Military Times reported that VA Undersecretary for Benefits Allison Hickey was concerned that even using the term "Gulf War illness" "might imply a causal link between service in the Gulf and poor health which could necessitate legislation for disability compensation for veterans who served in the Gulf." http://archive.militarytimes.com/article/20140422/BENEFITS04/ 304220036/Top-VA-official-questions-use-term-Gulf-War-illness-

She also recently testified to Congress that VA would meet its 2015 claims processing target of 125 days unless she had to add a quarter million new claims to her inventory overnight, as happened in 2010 when Agent Orange coverage was expanded: "That will kill us." http://www.veterans.senate.gov/hearings/va-claims-system-review-of-vas-transformation-progress [1:38:50 mark]

While VA says that it provides care and benefits to veterans suffering from Gulf War illness under the category "undiagnosed illnesses," http:// www.publichealth.va.gov/exposures/gulfwar/medically-unexplained-illness.asp, the reality is otherwise. A 2014 VA report to Congress revealed that only 11,216 Gulf War-related claims have been approved, while 80 percent are denied. http:// www.scribd.com/doc/241661207/Binns-Parting-Thoughts-093014, page 7. VA's September 2014 press release that "nearly 800,000 Gulf War era Veterans are receiving compensation benefits for service-connected issues" is grossly misleading. http:// www.91outcomes.com/2014/09/va-press-release-va-secretary-mcdonald.html VA counts every veteran in the area from 1990 to the present as "Gulf War era," not just those who served in 1990–91.

We are appalled that the government has been able to influence the workings of the Institute of Medicine, the most revered institution in American medical science, to further its shameful campaign to manipulate science to deny veterans care and benefits. Regrettably, however, we are not surprised, as this has been more common than not where Gulf War veterans' health has been concerned. For example:

1. For fourteen years, in response to a law passed by Congress in 1998, VA has ordered and the IOM has prepared reports on the health effects of thirty-three toxic substances to which Gulf War veterans were exposed. The law repeatedly specified that the reports must consider studies in both humans and in animals. For fourteen years, however, these IOM reports have considered only human studies. To do this, VA and the IOM not only have had to disregard the law; they also had to manipulate the standard established in the IOM reports on Agent Orange, inserting the word "human" in the standard. As a result, since most research studies of toxic substances are necessarily done in animals, these IOM Gulf War reports have never found sufficient evidence of an association between these substances and Gulf War veterans' health problems. In turn, VA has never recognized any toxic exposure as a reason for granting these ill veterans care and benefits. https://veterans.house.gov/ witness-testimony/james-h-binns-0

2. The most egregious of these IOM Gulf War reports was the Updated Literature Review of Sarin, in which animal studies were not considered even though new ani-

mal studies were the only reason that then-Secretary Principi ordered the report. The outcome of the report was predetermined before the VA–IOM contract was ever signed, by understandings between VA and IOM staff discussed in a cover letter from the then executive director of the IOM to the then head of the VA Environmental Agents Service. https://veterans.house.gov/witness-testimony/james-h-binns-0

3. The Research Advisory Committee recommended in 2008 that these IOM reports be redone in accordance with the law. http://www.va.gov/RAC–GWVI/docs/Committee—Documents/GWIandHealthofGWVeterans—RAC–GWVIReport—2008.pdf, pages 53–55, 57. However, they have not been redone. Worse, the manipulated standard is now being employed in VA-ordered IOM studies of the health of post-9/11 veterans. The 2011 IOM report on the long-term health effects of burn pits used to incinerate waste in Iraq and Afghanistan used the manipulated Gulf War standard (limited to human studies), not the Agent Orange standard. As a consequence, the IOM burn pits committee found "inadequate/insufficient evidence of an association between exposure to combustion products and cancer, respiratory disease, circulatory disease, neurologic disease, and adverse reproductive and developmental outcomes." http://books.nap.edu/openbook.php?record—id=13209&page=6

4. In 2006, the IOM did a general Gulf War literature review for VA, similar to the current task. Most of the report was a straightforward summary of the research, but IOM's press release and press conference focused on one conclusion that echoed the familiar government theme that there is "no unique Gulf War syndrome." Technically, this only means that others have similar symptoms, but the press release and conference spun the message to imply that Gulf War veterans have no major health problem. http://www.nbcnews.com/id/14801666/ns/health-health—care/t/study-gulf-war-syndrome-doesnt-exist/#.VHLDjUuBNH8

5. The 2013 IOM treatments report was a recent glaring example of VA and IOM collaboration to disregard the law and promote the 1990's government position. A 2010 law required VA to contract with the IOM for a comprehensive review of the best treatments for ill Gulf War veterans by a group of doctors experienced in treating Gulf War veterans "diagnosed with chronic multisymptom illness or another health condition related to chemical and environmental exposures that may have occurred during [their] service."

Instead, VA contracted for a literature review of treatments for all "populations with a similar constellation of symptoms," and the IOM appointed a committee with no experience in treating Gulf War veterans but extensive experience in psychiatric and psychosomatic medicine—though the 2010 IOM report had just concluded that the illness "cannot be ascribed to any known psychiatric disorder." Analysishttps://veterans.house.gov/sites/republicans.veterans.house.gov/files/Binns%2C%20ExhibitBtestimony.pdf http://www.scribd.com/doc/150949964/WHITE—PAPER–IOM–CMI–Panel-Membership-

The individuals selected to give background briefings to the committee were largely familiar advocates for the 1990's position, who told the committee the problem was psychiatric. http://www.va.gov/RAC—GWVI/docs/Committee—Documents/CommitteeDocJune2012.pdf, pages 24–30. Half the illnesses whose therapies were reviewed were psychiatric. The report revived 1990's themes that that "[t]hroughout modern history, many soldiers returning from combat have experienced postcombat illnesses. . . that cannot now be attributed to any diagnosable pathophysiologic entity or disease," and that "[c]linicians should approach [chronic multisymptom illness] with 'a person-centered model of care . . . that helps patients understand that the word psychosomatic is not pejorative.'" https://veterans.house.gov/sites/republicans.veterans.house.gov/files/Binns%2C%20ExhibitBtestimony.pdf

6. The person who identified the individuals to be invited to brief the treatment committee was the chief scientist of the VA Office of Public Health, according to Congressional testimony by a senior VA epidemiologist who worked for him. https://veterans.house.gov/witness-testimony/dr-steven-s-coughlin

7. One of the psychiatric-oriented briefers was a member of the IOM Board on the Health of Select Populations, the IOM board that oversees veterans' studies. Dr. Kurt Kroenke, an Army doctor and psychiatric-oriented Gulf War researcher in the 1990's, is a leading figure in somatic medicine. He co-chaired the "Conceptual Issues in Somatoform and Similar Disorders" project that laid the groundwork for the controversial expansion of the definition of somatoform disorders in the recently revised Diagnostic and Statistical Manual of Mental Disorders (DSM–5) of the American Psychiatric Association. http://www.ncbi.nlm.nih.gov/pubmed/17600162 http://dxrevisionwatch.com/dsm-5-drafts/dsm-5-ssd-work-group/ He has co-authored publications with two members of the IOM treatment committee and two members of the new IOM committee that begins work December 3.

8. Two other members of the IOM Board of the Health of Select Populations were also leading proponents of the government position on Gulf War health in the

1990's. Dr. Francis Murphy held the position equivalent to chief scientist in VA's Office of Public Health, and Dr. Greg Gray was a Navy doctor who published numerous papers in 1996–2001 that dismissed the idea that Gulf War veterans have any special health problems. Conversely, as of June 2013, no one on the IOM Board of the Health of Select Populations represented current scientific understanding of Gulf War illness. http://www.scribd.com/doc/150949964/WHITE–PAPER–IOM–CMI–Panel-Membership-Analysis. It is currently undisclosed who serves on this board, as its membership has been removed from the IOM website, although the membership of all other IOM boards continues to be listed. http://www.iom.edu/About-IOM/Leadership-Staff/Boards.aspx

In summary, there has been a long-term corrupt relationship between the government and the Institute of Medicine to deny the true state of Gulf War veterans' health, of which the makeup of the new committee is only the latest example.

We are confident that neither you nor VA Secretary McDonald, as newcomers to Washington and to your respective institutions, is aware of this problem. At one point, none of us would have believed it possible either. But it is a cancer that threatens to destroy the integrity and reputations of both organizations. And it makes a mockery of the mission of the IOM "to provide unbiased and authoritative advice to decision makers and the public." http://www.iom.edu/About-IOM.aspx

We urge you to conduct a thorough investigation of this problem and to fix it. The most effective and rapid approach is for the IOM to handle this itself. If it does not, however, we will work with veterans' organizations to show Congress the need to conduct an investigation and enact legislative solutions.

As part of putting IOM on solid ground going forward, we urge you to replace the eight provisional members predisposed to the government's scientifically discredited 1990's position with individuals representing current scientific knowledge of Gulf War research and the health effects of neurotoxic exposures. We also urge you to replace those members of the Board on the Health of Select Populations identified with this position, with individuals representing current scientific knowledge regarding veterans' health and environmental exposures.

Respectfully,

James Binns
Former Chairman, Research Advisory Committee on Gulf War Veterans Illnesses

Beatrice A. Golomb, MD, PhD
Professor of Medicine, University of California San Diego

Current Member, Research Advisory Committee; former Committee Scientific Director

Rev. Joel C. Graves, DMin,
CPT U.S. Army (Ret.)
Former Member, Research Advisory Committee

Marguerite L. Knox, MN, ARNP–FNP/ACNP
COL, South Carolina Army National Guard
Former Member, Research Advisory Committee

William J. Meggs, MD, PhD
Professor and Chief, Division of Toxicology, Brody School of Medicine, East Carolina University
Former Member, Research Advisory Committee

cc: Institute of Medicine Council

Analysis of the Provisional Committee Membership
November, 2014

The provisional committee is grossly imbalanced in favor of the 1990's government position that Gulf War veterans have no special health problem-just what happens after every war, related to psychiatric issues, and not environmental exposures.

The following committee members are predisposed toward this position, either because they personally supported it, or because they are professionally oriented to view these kinds of health problems as psychiatric and unrelated to environmental exposures.

Dr. Kenneth Kizer, as VA Undersecretary for Health, 1994–1999, was the chief promulgator of this position, including this 1997 Congressional testimony: "The overall frequency of unexplained symptoms among Gulf War veterans appears to be about the same as in a general medical practice." http://www.va.gov/OCA/testimony/hvac/sh/hvac61.asp

Dr. Howard Kipen, a member of the VA Persian Gulf Expert Scientific Committee, 1993–1997, has published "Military deployment to the Gulf War as a risk factor for psychiatric illness among U.S. troops" (2005) http://bjp.rcpsych.org/content/188/5/453.long and that "[c]oncerns . . . of a unique Gulf War syndrome, remind us that military personnel returning from wars have regularly described disabling symptoms" (co-authored with Dr. Kroenke). Unexplained Symptoms after Terrorism and War: An Expert Consensus Statement. Journal of Occupational and Environmental Medicine 45(10):1040–8, 2003

Dr. Herman Gibb runs a private consulting firm. The NIH reportedly terminated its contract with his previous firm, while he was president, on grounds that his firm was working for three chemical companies at the same time it was reviewing their chemicals for the government. http://www.washingtonpost.com/wp-dyn/content/article/2007/04/13/AR2007041301979.html

Dr. Nancy Woods is an expert on midlife and aging women's health; her background relevant to Gulf War illness was as a member of the IOM committee that authored a 1996 report, "The Health Consequences of Service During the Persian Gulf War," which concluded: "Men and women served side by side in conditions that increased the stresses of serving in these grim surroundings . . . Studies of Gulf War veterans suggest that these veterans suffer from a variety of recognized diseases, . . . not the existence of a new disease. " http://books.nap.edu/openbook.php?record—id=5272&page=R6

Dr. Javier Escobar is a professor of psychiatry at the Robert Wood Johnson Medical School, where his work "focuses on the somatic presentations of psychiatric disorders in primary care . . . as director of the 'Medically Unexplained Physical Symptoms Research Center.'" http://www.physicianfacultyscholars.org/nac/escobar.html With Dr. Kroenke he was a member of the "Conceptual Issues in Somatoform and Similar Disorders" project that laid the groundwork for the controversial expansion of the definition of somatoform disorders in the recently revised Diagnostic and Statistical Manual of Mental Disorders (DSM–5) of the American Psychiatric Association, and was a member of the task force that wrote DSM–5. http://www.ncbi.nlm.nih.gov/pubmed/17600162 http://dxrevisionwatch.com/dsm-5-drafts/dsm-5-ssd-work-group/ http://www.dsm5.org/MeetUs/Pages/TaskForceMembers.aspx He was a member of the 2013 IOM treatment report committee.

Dr. Scott Fishman is board certified in psychiatry and pain medicine. His research includes a focus on "psychiatric issues of chronic illness and pain." http://www.ucdmc.ucdavis.edu/publish/facultybio/search/faculty/508

Dr. Alberto Caban-Martinez studies musculoskeletal pain in workers related to their occupational risk factors. http://www.cabanmartinezlab.com/#!about/c46c He has studied "The prevalence of Somatic Disfunctions in a Multi-Center Outpatient Osteopathic Medicine Clinic" http://nhsn.med.miami.edu/documents/cv/a—cabanmartinez—cv—09.pdf and has published that "[c]onstruction workers struggle with a high prevalence of mental distress, and this is associated with their pain and injuries." J Occup Environ Med 2013 Oct;55(10):1197–204

Dr. Deborah Cory-Slecta, the committee chair, has not done Gulf War health research herself but stated in 2013, in connection with service on another IOM Gulf War committee, that she does not believe Gulf War illness research has produced adequate data to show what caused the illness. http://www.forbes.com/sites/rebeccaruiz/2014/03/12/experts-cant-decide-on-definition-for-gulf-war-illness/ She also served on the 2003 IOM Gulf War committee that concluded there was insufficient evidence to show an association between any illness affecting Gulf War veterans and exposure to pesticides, applying the manipulated standard that excluded animal studies. http://www.nap.edu/openbook.php?record—id=10628&page=R5

The other half of the committee are neutral, people who have not been engaged in Gulf War health research themselves, but who have a background in studying other neurological conditions and expertise in relevant subjects like neuroimaging, neuropsychology, and neuroepidemiology. They include Dr. Robert Brown, Dr. Ellen Eisen, Dr. Mary Fox, Dr. Clifford Jack, Dr. Joel Kramer, Dr. Francine Laden, Dr. James Noble, and Dr. Anbesaw Selassie.

Conspicuously absent from the committee are any doctors or scientists who have studied Gulf War health in the past decade, who have studied or treated other groups subjected to neurotoxic exposures like farmers or pesticide applicators, or who have studied the effects of Gulf War exposures in animals.

MONTRA DENISE NICHOLS

Submitted by Montra Denise Nichols, MAJ USAFR(RET), RN(ret), MSN

Vice Chair of National Vietnam and Gulf War Veterans Coalition

Good afternoon Committee members and Veterans. I am Montra Denise Nichols,Maj, Retired USAF NURSE, Gulf War veteran and Vice Chairman of National Vietnam and Gulf War Veterans Coalition. I am also one of the ill gulf war veterans. I have attended all but two of the VA RAC GWIR meetings except for 2, attended all the VA advisory committee meetings on Gulf War Health and Benefits, have attended in person or by phone the IOM NAS public meetings on GWI, served on the first DOD–CDMRP Peer review process at DOD CDMRP, PAC meetings, PSOB meeting, town hall meetings by OSIGWI meetings, CDC meeting in 1999, hearings on the hill and have testified in person or by written submission since 1994, and in addition have attended medical conferences that have direct connections to our illnesses. I have also participated in 8 research projects as a research subject for 6 researchers on gulf war illness. Ialso was listed as a coauthor on the Hypercoagulation peer reviewed paper published in 2000.

Over the last 22 years since our return home from Operation Desert Storm we have continued to advocate for all gulf war veterans that are ill. It has been a long trudge through this mass of activity and now our journey that seems to have a perpetual loop between VA , Institute of Medicine reports from the National Academy of Science, hearings here on the hill on an irregular basis, and the VA RAC GWIR. It is disappointing to say the least that the situation never seems to get on the Right Path to unify and address the real physical damage that veterans of Operation Desert Storm encountered after toxic exposures. The VA RAC GWIR and the DOD CDMRP has been the leaders in this effort to get answers thru real medical research to find the right diagnostic tests, biomarkers and finally real treatment options that are not palliative. The VA seems to be the road block over and over. The veterans of the gulf war are suffering because of the Actions of the VA or shall I say the INACTION. I have witnessed first hand how the VA RAC GWIR Advisory committee has labored since 2002 and have seen the intransigent activity of the VA. This is occurring at the top and seen clearly at the bottom re the clinical care of the gulf war veterans or the lack thereof and there is a problem that has not been solved for 22 years. I left the VA angry when my female hematologist primary care told me her hands were tied, and she even got tears in her eyes. I left because I both in the information on the hypercoagulation problem that I feel as a nurse can relate to early needless deaths of gulf war veterans who are ill. I had my own test results and she would not call the Drs and researchers that had done this study independently. They were concerned about my own elevated values and had suggested treatment that she refused to consider. What really made me madder was when I found out the editor of that journal that published our peer review research was the head of the VA lab at the Denver VA the one I was going to for care. That was in 2000. Since then I have tried to go back to the VA and told during 2003–4 time period it would take 6 months to a year to get an appointment. I continued as many of us have to suffered and seek care when I could. I was lucky to have health care insurance through my husband but I lived in fear of loosing it if they the doctors deemed it war related. I certainy did not want to risk the insurance we had for my husband and my child. I struggle finding doctors that want to delve into this because they also do not have the knowledge on toxic exposure effects and they are hesitant to get involved when their might be government forces at work. I know the doctors that have suffered retaliation from the VA for trying to help, I know some of the researchers that are hesitant also because of that same potential, and we even had a county corner fired when she ruled a death of a veteran due to gulf war exposures. I have had a benefactor that helped several veterans get care through environmental medicine doctors, and I return to them when I can afford to travel and pay out of pocket for their fees and tests. I know of other civilian doctors I would like to get to but again it involves travel and cost factors. I was recruited for research at WRIIS at DC and received good research testing and caring doctors but yet they did not put me through the 2 day WRIIS protocol. I have said I will pay for my travel but I want to get thru that evaluation, I am being denied that until I can get back into the VA medical appointment system in Denver and get a doctor to refer me to WRIIS. And since what I got was research those test have not been entered in my record, I was told yes I failed the testing which to me was no big surprise. But it doesn't help with getting further care or a claim that is service connected.

I have participated in research projects and even recruited others to participate and know the researchers are finding clues and when their papers are published ·those results will help hopefully to better diagnosis and treatment potentials. But when doctors are not being educated on those findings then the interface with research and care is failing.

We the veterans see the continued battles that have occurred thru the years. It is a shame and a disgrace that the VA has not taken the advice of the RAC GWIR. That interference has stymied for years the beneficial work of scientific researchers, doctors, and researchers. It has blocked actively the improvements that could of have been made over the last 22 years in the actual clinical care that could have made a difference in the quality of care, diagnostic abilities, and yes real treatment. And yes they could have saved countless lives of gulf war veterans that have died in an early age group under the age of 50!

I was one of roughly 20 fellow veterans that took part in the public meetings of the last IOM/NAS report. Each offered public comment and offered the IOM committee real insight into our situation. ALL of us were in anguish listening to their first public meeting that concentrated on the psychology-stress aspect yet again! After listening, then offering public comment, and debriefing with my fellow ill veterans and spouses that were on line, I immediately called the chairman of the VA RAC GWIR, Mr. Binns. I wanted to give him our feedback, what had been covered, and our very deep concerns that this marked yet again a back tracking effort on the part of the VA that institutes the charter and guidance when they contract a literature review from the IOM/NAS. It was like all the work that had been done on gulf war illness research had not even been considered.

Our input seemed to not even be heard. These committee members I wonder if they have ever seen and cared for even 100 of the gulf war vets with the multitude of health issues. After 22 years and excellent research from outstanding doctors and researchers that had proven that physical damage has occurred to hundreds of thousands of veterans it appeared we were back to step one all over again. The IOM/NAS never ever in their hearings heard presentations from the doctors and researchers that have studied us or group of gulf war veterans to be able to comprehend their findings. This is wrong.

Their definition the IOM committee used is so broad that it creates confusion yet again. Patients that have had chemotherapy could easily fit the definition and have had no military exposures much less other categories of patients. This definition does not even have relevance to the definitions already being used for the RAC GWIR reports of 04-thru current year. They did not even utilize guidance that the DOD CDMRP process has used since 2006 in peer review and awarding of gulf war illness research. Their definition truly creates havoc in the work that has been developed by researchers over the past 10 years. The IOM NAS committee did not hear from the range of researchers that have been involved thru the years examples include UTSW Medical , Wright State, University of Miami, to name just a few.

Again and again the VA and IOM/NAS work seems to set us further behind in the goals to get better diagnostic testing of gulf war veterans who have suffered for 22 yrs. The goal of getting true treatment gets pushed back yet again. Right now we basically have COQ10(that the VA hospitals will not provide) and CPAP (used in sleep apnea) as real physical treatment. I put acupuncture and cognitive behavior techniques as supportive palliative treatment. As an analogy I would use a cardiac patient with significant blockages of the cardiac arteries that need stents/bypass/medications being ordered to just use exercise, acupuncture, and stress reduction as their total care. The situation is dire.

More and more of the results from research are showing significant damage to the brain and the autonomic nervous system. This should help make sense of what health care providers are seeing at each VA hospital. When you have brain and autonomic nervous system and hypercoagulation of the blood involved it affects every other organ in the body.

The care of our gulf war veterans is impacted by the VA that still resists the significance of the damage done to hundreds of thousands of gulf war veterans. When the doctors and health care providers are not updated/educated on all the significance findings of this effort in research it is truly unacceptable. When the veteran patient/client is even providing hand carried copies of the reports and research papers to their health care provider at the VA and for those efforts to be ignored is truly showing some type of mind set to ignore, delay, and deny. The VA even when they have misspent money on conferences in the past number of years have not even focused on education for the clinicians on what is being found in research on gulf war illness and seeking to institute a true intergradation of research into the clinical practice of health care providers that are seeing the gulf war veterans who are ill daily. Legislation is needed.

The clinicians on the whole don't even know of the WRIISC and the referral method that shows you why most veterans give their health care provider a D or F in grading. The clinicians could also be asked to give feedback to the RAC GWIR or headquarters VA Health care on information and findings they are finding on their gulf war veterans but that is not done. There is no interface between the VA health care providers and the Researchers and Doctors that have worked with gulf war veterans in civilian or VA practice. This needs urgent action at the highest priority!

It is unconscionable to see that some gulf war veterans have found civilian doctors and resources that can do testing and help gulf war veterans but the majority of gulf war veterans cannot pay out of their pocket to travel and get to these doctors and pay those civilian doctors. WE know there are places like the Mayo Clinic that can provide autonomic nervous system testing but 99% cannot get that important testing. The VA has not had training programs or the equipment in order to perform this testing. There is now a commercially available test for the hypercoagulation problem that was first researched and published in 2000, and we have research currently on that area by Dr. Bach at VA Minneapolis on this topic. Again a critical need that could possibly save gulf war veterans lives from pulmonary embolism, cardiac incidents, strokes, deep vein thrombus, and other death potential diagnoses. Where is the priority to truly help gulf war veterans and get the diagnostic testing and lifesaving treatment? Legislation is needed.

Then we have only 3 WRIIS serving as second opinion but there are hundreds of thousands of gulf war veterans not getting the highest quality of care that should be available at each VA hospital or at least one in each VA region. The majority of the veterans asked said their VA primary care personnel had no knowledge of gulf war related illnesses and physical problems. The veterans that gave an A or a B were the ones that had gotten to the WRIIS or had struggled to get a change of doctor or a referral to a specialist like rheumatology. (these are still in the low minority , seeing that the WRIIS only see limited number of gulf war veterans(2 a week)) . When asked to grade the education of the providers on exposures and effects, gulf war illness, and care from the VA providers the grades given were predominately D and F.

Additionally care also involves helping the spouse or loved one trying to take care of the veteran at home. Unfortunately, although we served in Iraq as did the current OIF, OEF veterans no provision was made to cover caregivers for the Operation Desert Storm Veterans of 1990–91. A percentage of our veterans need that help too! The spouses are suffering and trying to be the bread winners of the family while caring for their adult veteran spouse that have become housebound to varying degrees. With the significant neurocognitive, the debilitating CFIDS, or development of MS, Cancers, or other devastating illnesses in a group of younger veterans below the age of 50 there needs to be consideration to including the spouses from 1990–91 who may still have young children school age at home(and some of these have developmental type problems.) The door to caregiver assistance needs to be consider for these cases including ALS veterans. Legislative effort will be needed to amend that law.

The need is there for the providers of health care in the VA to have the gulf war veterans seen by designated trained physicians at each VA hospital/clinic. WE need our gulf war clinics back that we had in the nineties. WE need to have support groups at each VA hospital for gulf war veterans and their spouses with care providers and social workers. WE need gulf war veteran task forces at each VA or at least at one VA hospital in the state to have the interaction that is needed to be heard and improvements made. Legislation will be needed.

WE need an active sharing of data on deaths, age, unit, cause of death and statistics in comparison to the normal non- military age groups. This is needed for our researchers and for us the veterans. This will need legislation.

WE need a robust accounting like we had with GWVIS data that is produced every three months. The data needs to show diagnoses and ages. Again researchers and veterans need this information. Legislation will be needed.

WE need to have you all reconsider registry for the family members that feel their symptoms are the same as the veterans. WE had that in the ninties but it was allowed to expire time wise. Again legislation needed.

WE need the VA to hire consultants in the area of environmental medicine and integrative medicine to be involved in updating the VA system in dealing with exposures effects. Again legislation will be needed.

WE need all data from the DOD declassified. It has been 22yrs and some of that massive data could possible provide insights into the potential causes. This may have a direct impact on our health. Again legislation is needed.

WE need newsletters that are not just PR pieces for the VA but informative and that includes all research findings and recruitment not just from VA research but DOD CDMRP research or other civilian research that might match conditions/diagnoses that the veterans are receiving. Legislation is needed.

WE need our records clearly identified as Gulf War in theater or non-deployed and unit assigned to in order to also have data that would show if particular units are more ill or have a higher death rate. Legislation will be needed,

Our veterans are actively seeking a means to relocate their fellow veterans that served in the same unit. There should be a means to help veterans to find each other to facilitate buddy letters if needed. And this would also assist our researchers. Legislation is needed.

The other item is to provide fee basis to get the testing that is commercially available ie hypercoagulation test . The need for autonomic nervous system testing that the VA cannot provide needs to be funded not only for those in the VA system but those other gulf war veterans not being seen at the VA. Specific legislation is needed.

There needs to be another time period extended for gulf war veterans that missed the initial time period allowed after operation desert storm or those that got fed up and left the VA and have struggled to find help in the civilian medical field. Currently I am living through that and have had a number of veterans communicate with me this past week of not being allowed in VA if they did not meet the means test. Much less those with insurance that they paid for being billed for health effects of service while they continue to try to get their claims through the system. Legislation is needed.

The VA still wants to label this with a name or diagnosis that does not even relate to military, war time, or hazardous exposures and that in itself is viewed as an insult to the veterans! The VA still wants to push treatment that centers on Psychological and stress, we deserve better. We started out with many VA gulf war clinics in the nineties and then they were closed! Legislation is needed.

The gulf war veterans when they try to discuss their exposures and relationship to their service and effect on changes in their body systems with their health care provider they are verbally or nonverbally shut down. We gulf war veterans have guided other veterans experiencing these problems to ask for change of doctors or provider at VA and we have provided the education to the veterans about the WRIIS program and guided them to inform and educate their doctor of the information on the VA's own website about the WRIIS and how the doctors are to refer them electronically. Legislation is needed for mandatory CME education for our health providers seeing ill gulf war veterans. Legislation is needed.

We have provided the flow of information even the actual research papers and RAC GWIR reports to our fellow gulf war veterans and encouraged them to share it with their VA health care providers. We have done the outreach to the veterans not the VA, we do this as our continued duty to each other as former military personnel that do care for each other even when we have not met them in person. WE listen and read what they are experiencing and their frustrations at getting sicker and having less quality of life and do our best to try to help our fellow gulf war veterans even as we are also ill and struggling to get care that we deserve.

WE have tried but as you see after 22 years we need firm legislative efforts and laws that will be enforced to make a difference!

And most of all the VA RAC GWIR needs to be recognized and VA must be held accountable for their intransience that has led to poor diagnostic testing, biomarker development, care and potential breakthroughs for treatment. This must stop. And the cycle ongoing between VA and IOM NAS must be but under great scrutiny.

WE also need hearings more frequently with the House and Senate VA committees. I suggest joint hearings to elevate the priority and to gain unity on the hill on this effort. I also suggest that other gulf war veterans and a few spouses be allowed to testify to truly give more insight to our elected representatives of what we are living through. WE also need an ongoing VA advisory committee on health and benefits for gulf war veterans in law so it is not a one time 18 month advisory committee. These issues need just as much attention as the Research. Legislation similar to the legislation that set up the VA RAC GWIR is needed. Until the situation is improved we need this effort. WE need transparency and reports publicly available for any and all Task Force activities concerning gulf war veterans' illnesses that VA has conducted! Please legislate and enforce these efforts so direly needed. Our claims are likewise in poor condition because VSO's and VA rating officials have not been trained to adequately deal with the claims of gulf war illnesses. WE need urgent help 22 years is too long to have waited.

☛

KIMBERLY SULLIVAN, PHD

25 Years after the Gulf War: Gulf War Illness, Brain Cancer and Future Research

Research Assistant Professor, Department of Environmental Health
Boston University School of Public Health

Former Associate Scientific Director
VA Research Advisory Committee on Gulf War Veterans' Illnesses

On this week marking the 25th anniversary of the Gulf War, I would like to express my concern and disappointment with the conclusions from the recent volume 10 Institute of Medicine Gulf War Report and highlight some of the important research that is ongoing in this field.

Gulf War Illness

GWI is a constellation of chronic health symptoms including fatigue, pain, headaches, gastrointestinal and cognitive problems. It is a multi-system disorder meaning that it affects not only the central nervous system but also the immune and gastrointestinal systems. It affects about a third of the nearly 700,000 veterans deployed to the war.

Gulf War Illness as a Functional Disorder

The IOM report goes to great length to describe GWI as a self-reported symptom based disorder for which there are no current objective biomarkers and therefore it must be a 'functional disorder' meaning it has no physical cause. The report describes it to be similar to other well accepted symptom based disorders including post-traumatic stress disorder (PTSD). In fact, this report places PTSD as the only disorder that has 'sufficient evidence of causal association' to deployment to the Gulf War while it places GWI in the second category of 'sufficient evidence of an association' to deployment to the Gulf War.

However, less than 10% of GW veterans have been diagnosed with PTSD and more than 30% have been diagnosed with GWI. In addition, it is completely unclear why GWI is not also causally-related to deployment to the war when both disorders are diagnosed the same way - by self-report of chronic health symptoms.

The report also stresses that the health conditions associated with Gulf War deployment are primarily mental health disorders and functional medical disorders and that these associations emphasize the interconnectedness of the brain and body.

However, the brain and body are interconnected in GWI not because this is a stress-related disorder without a unifying pathobiological cause as the IOM report suggests, but rather because they are all part of the brain and immune pathways that are activated as part of the neuroinflammatory response to pesticide and nerve agent exposures. These chemicals directly target the nervous system and cause inflammation. These pathways start by activating the immune cells in the brain called microglia that release chemical messengers called cytokines in the brain and the many body systems that are affected in GWI. Activating these inflammatory systems in the brain and throughout the body can result in chronic symptoms such as joint and muscle pain, memory problems, fatigue, headaches, and gastrointestinal distress-all symptoms found in GWI. Researchers call this type of chronic condition a post-inflammatory brain syndrome.

In fact, a paper by Gulf War researchers from the Centers for Disease Control (CDC) recently showed that Gulf War-relevant pesticides and nerve agents produced a neuroinflammatory response resulting in hundreds-fold higher cytokine chemical signaling in a GWI animal model. Preliminary studies in veterans with GWI suggest increased cytokine levels that correlate with GWI symptoms as well.

Treatment focus for Veterans with GWI

The IOM report has concluded that research efforts should be realigned to focus on the treatment and 'management' of Gulf War illness rather than its causes. However, biological targets focused on neuroinflammatory markers described above provide tangible and targeted treatment strategies for GWI. Researchers at Boston University, Nova Southeastern University and VA medical centers in Boston, Bronx and Miami are currently assessing the effectiveness of targeted treatment trials using intranasal insulin, D-cycloserine and Co-enzyme Q10 to treat the constellation of symptoms in GWI including cognitive, fatigue and pain symptoms. Clinical researchers can do better for our veterans than 'manage' their symptoms as the IOM suggests and the research community is hopeful that these currently funded treatments will provide much needed symptom relief for ill Gulf War veterans.

Brain Cancer Association with Gulf War Service

The IOM report also states that the results of two published VA studies reporting significantly increased brain cancer mortality rates found in GW veterans who were in close proximity to the Khamisiyah weapons depot detonations where large stores of sarin/cyclosarin were destroyed cannot be trusted because the exposure plume modelling done to determine who was exposed may be inaccurate. However, inaccuracies in exposure modeling often make the analysis less sensitive rather than more sensitive to finding differences between groups. Therefore, finding a 2 and 3 fold increase in brain cancer deaths in sarin exposed GW veterans suggests that these rates are likely an underestimate of effect rather than an overestimate of the effect of sarin exposure on brain cancer mortality in GW veterans.

Conclusion

The IOM report has downplayed the importance of continuing to research the remaining questions in GWI including identifying biomarkers of current illness, prior neutoxicant exposures and targeted treatment strategies. This work is critically important to Gulf War veterans who suffer from chronic health effects from these toxicant exposures but also for many others including those who are occupationally exposed to pesticides, including farmers and pesticide applicators around the world. Gulf War veterans are counting on researchers to identify the cause and pathobiology of their debilitating illness, and to identify treatments that will work to improve all of their symptoms, not just manage them.

Most importantly, the end result of this report is that GW veterans suffering from brain cancer or family members of those who have already succumbed to brain cancer will not receive VA benefits now or likely ever for their service-related mortality. These veterans have been forced to fight for benefits while they are fighting for their lives. These veterans should be given the benefit of the doubt in providing them with VA service connection for this service-related mortality.

☛

DAVID K. WINNETT, II

Thank you, Chairman Coffman, Ranking Member Kuster, and Members of the House Veterans' Affairs Subcommittee on Oversight and Investigations for today's hearing.

I also wish to thank my fellow brothers- and sisters-in-arms who have joined this hearing in person, and to those of my fellow Persian Gulf War veterans who are watching these proceedings from afar. The testimony I provide to this distinguished Committee is done in honor of the extraordinary sacrifices that my fellow Gulf War veterans have made over the course of the past 25 years, first by the historic and heroic victory achieved during the 1991 Persian Gulf War, and then by the super human sacrifices made in the years since, both individually and collectively, in fighting what has turned out to be a much more formidable foe than the enemy soldiers we once routed on the toxic battlefields of the Middle East.

BACKGROUND

I am a 20-year veteran of the United States Marine Corps, having enlisted as a Private in January 1975 and retiring as Captain in 1995. In total, I wore 11 different ranks as a Marine, from Private (E1) through Staff Sergeant (E6), Warrant Officer (W1) through Chief Warrant Officer (W3), then First Lieutenant (earned while deployed to the Gulf) to Captain.

My service as a Marine was, without exception, the most rewarding experience of my life. I appear before this honorable body today, exactly 25 years to the day that I led a Platoon of the most courageous and capable United States Marines I ever had the honor of serving with across the line of departure into Kuwait, along with combat elements of the 1st Marine Division, to liberate that beleaguered country and its people from the occupying grip of a vicious dictator. As history now demonstrates, our mission succeeded well beyond what even the most educated military scholars had predicted earlier.

But sadly, I appear here before this Committee in many respects, a physically broken man. Not as a result of the normal aging process, not from the effects of enemy bullets or shrapnel, and certainly not from the stress of combat operations that occurred 25 years ago, but because of a physiological demon that managed to find a way to penetrate not only the substantial layers of protective clothing and equipment that I wore throughout the ground assault through Kuwait, but into my flesh, my internal organs, and through the blood-brain barrier that normally serves to protect the neurological mechanisms that control our cognitive abilities, our autonomic nervous system, and just about everything in the brain that regulates normal functioning of the human body.

In short, I am, and have been a very physically sick man for the past 20-plus years. But the fact remains, I am here, I am still a United States Marine, and as far as I'm concerned I remain actively engaged in combat, as do hundreds of thousands of my fellow Gulf War veterans. The only thing that has changed over the

25 years that have passed since our rapid and resounding defeat of the Iraqi Army is that now we face a different foe, a foe much more resourceful and stubborn than even the toughest Iraqis that we faced during Operation Desert Storm. It pains me to admit that the battle we fight today is against some within the U.S. government - the same government that sent us to war in the first place.

Over the past few weeks I have read numerous media accounts and engaged in a number of discussions with my fellow veteran advocates regarding the recent report issued by the Institute of Medicine (IOM) entitled, "Gulf War and Health, Volume 10: Update of Health Effects of Service in the Gulf War." I cannot find words that are of sufficient power to express the disappointment I feel in the conclusions and recommendations contained in that report. Given the substantial body of scientific evidence that over the past decade has proven time and time again, beyond any doubt whatsoever, that Gulf War Illness is indeed a genuine physiological illness and that effective physiological treatments can likely be found, I simply cannot believe that the IOM made a 180-degree turn away from that science to a position that Gulf War Illness should now be treated primarily as "mind-body interconnectedness" - as if it were a mental disorder.

In the interests of providing context to my testimony, I would hope that my military record would serve to support my assertion that when I say that I am physically sick, that I know my own body, and that my health conditions are primarily physical and not psychological, that your Committee would take me at my word. As many of you know, within the ranks of our military, an officer's word is his or her solemn bond. And when I say that I am convinced beyond any doubt whatsoever that, as countless research studies have shown, more than 200,000 of my fellow Gulf War veterans are as sick or sicker than myself, that your honorable body will trust me on that count as well.

My military career was, by any measure, a quite successful one. Few United States Marines are able to wear 11 different ranks over a period of only 20 years. A four-star General has been promoted nine times, usually over a span of 30 or more years; I was promoted ten times in 20 years. Three of the five promotions I received as a young enlisted Marine were earned "meritoriously". This is not an easy accomplishment in the Marine Corps, I assure you. During my assignment to the Non-Commissioned Officers (NCO) school at Camp Hansen, Okinawa, I finished second out of a class of 39. As a Sergeant (E5) at the Staff NCO Academy at El Toro, I finished second out of a class of 59, most of whom were very seasoned Staff Sergeants (E6) and Gunnery Sergeants (E7), many of them current or former drill instructors. Three years following that I was among just 250 of 2,500 applicants Marine Corps-wide to receive an appointment to the rank of Warrant Officer (W1), and I completed the Warrant Officer Basic Course in Quantico in the top 10% of my class. Later, while under orders to the Marine Corps Degree Completion Program, I completed a Bachelor of Business Degree (BBA) Magna cum Laude. I worked hard for every single promotion or personal decoration that I received as a Marine. Not once in 20 years did I ever fail to achieve a score of First Class on my quarterly Physical Fitness Tests (PFT). I was a competitive shooter as a young Lance Corporal, competing in the 1976 Far East Division Matches. I was good at whatever I set my mind to do.

I've listed these career milestones, not as a means of pounding my chest, but to convey to your honorable body that in 20 years of service as a United States Marine, I was never considered a "quitter" or a "sick bay commando". I was a competitive person then, and that competitive spirit still lives in me this very day. In fact, were it not for the fighting spirit I learned as a United States Marine, I doubt very much that I would be sitting here today. The point I'm making is this: I am appealing to the honorable members of this distinguished committee to take this Marine at his word. I am not a malingerer. I am not a liar. I am not mentally disturbed. My physical pain is real, and it is severe. The profound fatigue that I live with day in and day out is not a psychosomatic disorder. More importantly, the more than 200,000 of my brothers- and sisters-in-arms who live with the same physical pain and fatigue and other symptoms that I live with are not imagining their illnesses. This preposterous idea that Gulf War Illness should be treated primarily with cognitive behavioral therapy, exercise, and psychiatric drugs as suggested in this new DOD/VA Clinical Practice Guideline as if it were a psychosomatic condition is not only ridiculous, it is highly offensive to the warriors whose lives have been literally destroyed as a result of serving on what was undoubtedly the most toxic battlefield American forces have served on in the history of this great country.

Four years ago my worsening physical condition forced me to walk away from a prestigious position as the Fleet Services Manager for the City of Torrance, California, where I managed a $12 million dollar budget, 36 employees, and a fleet of over 700 vehicles, and had a salary of over $120,000 per year, not counting benefits.

Does anyone believe that a rational individual would walk away from such a lucrative career in order to obtain an annual veteran's disability payment of $36,000 per year?

I have been a very vocal advocate for veterans suffering from Gulf War Illness since 2008. I've written a number of op-eds for various news publications around the country, participated in radio and television interviews about Gulf War Illness, and shared quite a few poems written to honor the sacrifices of my fellow veterans. I have been actively involved with the Congressionally Directed Medical Research Program (CDMRP) for Gulf War Illness treatment research for the past six years as a consumer reviewer at both tiers of the review process, first as a member of the Scientific Merit Review panels, and currently as a member of the Programmatic Panel. I believe very strongly in the unparalleled work of this treatment development program.

ONLINE GULF WAR ILLNESSES DISCUSSION GROUP

In 2009, I created one of the first Facebook pages focused on Gulf War Illness. It is a "closed" group that goes by the name of "Gulf War Illnesses". Today this discussion group has an active membership of nearly 10,000 veterans, family members, and a few others interested in helping with our cause. As the sole administrator for the group, I personally screen each applicant who wishes to join to ensure it remains focused on our core mission - providing a private forum where ill Gulf War veterans feel free to share sensitive information about their battles with Gulf War Illness and other life challenges that often go hand in hand with chronic illness.

Members of the Gulf War Illnesses group also post frequent updates regarding ongoing Gulf War Illness research and news articles that are relevant to our cause. We have a number of very experienced individuals who offer free VA claims advice to other members. But most importantly, we provide a forum where veterans suffering from the debilitating symptoms of Gulf War Illness can find a sense of empathy, camaraderie, and mutual support any time of the day or night.

SUICIDES. Sadly, and more frequently than I would have expected, we sometimes lose members to suicide. Our group is fiercely loyal and protective of one another. Anytime a veteran posts comments that are indicative of possible suicidal ideations, you can rest assured that there will be an instant and incredible outpouring of support aimed at that veteran, including, if necessary, calls to local public safety officials asking that they conduct a welfare check on our veteran. Unfortunately, as hard as we try, we've not always been successful. We've lost far too many of our members to suicide. The vast majority of them were directly triggered by the sense of hopelessness that often follows a veteran's notification from the VA that his or her claim has been denied. These tragedies must stop. Each and every veteran suicide is completely preventable. Only the Department of Veterans Affairs has the power to end this epidemic by improving the relevance of the healthcare they provide, reforming their claims processing, and by ensuring that every VA facility across this country is operating under the exact same protocols as every other VA facility, including healthcare facilities and VA Regional Offices where individual claims decisions are adjudicated.

SURVEY SHOWING VA AND IOM HAVE MISSED THE MARK. Very recently, I conducted an informal survey of sorts on the Gulf War Illnesses group about Gulf War veterans' physical health concerns being dismissed by VA in favor of mental health referrals. The response to that question was rapid and voluminous. Within the first 24 hours, I had nearly 300 responses, the majority of which verified my suspicions that indeed, this problem - that Gulf War veterans with physical health issues are sent to VA mental health instead of addressing their physical health issues - is widespread and extremely common in just about every region within VA's jurisdiction. In my opinion there is little doubt that this unethical practice is not just a Clinical Practice Guideline document written by DOD and VA officials, it has become standard operating procedure throughout the VA. Below is my question and a few of the responses:

"If you are a Veteran of the 1991 Persian Gulf War and are living with life-altering medical problems such as severe muscle or joint pain, profound fatigue, gastrointestinal dysfunction, chronic skin rash, cognitive difficulties, etc.....AND your complaints to VA Physicians have not been taken seriously, I have a question to ask you. Who among you, instead of being treated for your physical complaints at the VA have instead been referred for psychiatric or psychological treatment?"

□ **Veteran from Dallas, Texas** - "Even though I am diagnosed with chronic fatigue (CF), Fibromyalgia, and IBS, just to name a few; The VA still only treats me for mental health. And if they do that to me, I can only imagine what they are doing to others. My doctors used to think I was just a complainer because I knew too much about GWI, now I am lucky if I ever see a doctor. All they ever give me is nurse practitioners, and I don't know about you guys, but every time an NP checks me out, they spend all of their time trying to un-diagnose everything, and trying to tell me GWI is all in my head."

☐ **Veteran from Taylorsville, Kentucky** - "I was actually told by VA that there were no validated reports of illnesses related to the Gulf War."

☐ **Veteran from Muskogee, Oklahoma** - "During my last visit to the Muskogee VA ER I had a doctor inform me since they could not find anything in the X rays or blood test he was submitting a recommendation for mental evaluation and that Gulf War Illness was not real. .. If they have physical health conditions the doctors will minimize health issues because of the documented psychological problems and not do as many tests that may help them on down the road. I had many problems at Loma Linda VA. Most consults were denied. Eventually had to go outside VA for tests to prove conditions existed. I had to go through director to get MRI. The MRI showed severe deterioration condition. Need 2 surgeries. I believe most veterans will have real physical issues on down the road and will be managed by the less costly meds."

☐ **Veteran from Sturgis, Michigan** - "All my diagnosis [sic] were done [by] my private pcp . VA did nothing for me. I have also been on Zoloft since 93 for my depression tried suicide twice so been a long hard road."

☐ **Veteran from Tallahassee, Alabama** - "My late husband was referred for mental health testing six months or so before he passed in '99...dismissed all his complaints."

☐ **Veteran from Springfield, Missouri** - "My primary care provider says that my IBS, fatigue, sleep problems, etc. are all just PTSD. My deployment to [the Persian Gulf] was actually easier and more fun than stateside never had any traumatic experiences. Also I have never been diagnosed with PTSD, and the psychologist says I am not depressed, just frustrated with lack of help for my health problems."

☐ **Veteran from Korbel, California** - "I finally went into the VA 3 years ago because I could no longer afford an outside physician to treat symptoms of GWI and was immediately referred to psych and diagnosed PTSD and given a slew of placating meds. Fortunately I had already failed off of most of them and was persistent and finally I am getting them to treat my IBS neuropathy and fibromyalgia."

☐ **Veteran from Duncan, Oklahoma** - "Insomnia, chronic fatigue, skin rash, sleep apnea. And yes sent to the shrink and tried about 4 different medications each one [expletive] me up more than the previous. They said I was depressed within 5 minutes of appointment. The 2nd doc said I wasn't depressed just had insomnia, prescribed trazadone, which was the very 1st med my primary Dr. Tried. Right back to square one. I quit going. And as far as sleep goes, I find listening to an audio book is better than any of the meds I was on."

☐ **Veteran from Conyers, Georgia** - "My pcp told me she was [not] interested in my conspiracy theories, only my current health. X-rays put me in Phys therapy for my back. And she referred me to psych, where I was diagnosed with PTSD."

☐ **Veteran from Pine Island, Minnesota** - "I was referred to mental health after having pulmonary and cardio work-up. When I started this time around (in 2013) I called to see what I needed to do to be seen for the fatigue and the nurse, this was when I actually was able to call the clinic and not triage, was honest enough to tell me that I would have to see MH to rule out those possibilities. The psychiatrist is the one who actually made the call on CFS. She is also the one who told me a year later that she wasn't sure how I should be treated or what I wanted out of continuing seeing her. .. I think many in the VA have no idea what to do with undiagnosed, maybe [THEY] should be referred to MH to help them find out what is wrong with them that they cannot accept that the medical establishment has not been able to definitively establish a diagnosis."

☐ **Veteran from Hawthorne, Florida** - "Gainesville VA, mental hygiene is all they offer. Make ya think you're crazy. .. I'll never walk [through] a VA again willingly."

☐ **Veteran from Geneva, Ohio** - "I have but I can say that they put me on anxiety medication . that I have now been on for about 5 years and it has made some good changes for sleep for me but . my body still hurts all the time and have joint and back pain, . But still living with headaches almost daily as well and skin rashes with severe psoriasis and memory loss. Believe it or not as I'm writing this I have to stop for a bit to remember names of things that I have known for years, . this sucks especially when I have to ask my wife and she looks at me like "what the [expletive] is wrong with you" and I'm only 49."

☐ **Veteran from Louisville, Kentucky** - "My pcp told me it was because I am depressed and had PTSD."

☐ **Veteran from Parkersburg, West Virginia** - "When I first went to the local CBOC complaining of these issues I was referred to Psych. Later I was told all my problems were from PTSD."

☐ **Veteran from Topeka, Kansas** - "I was already seeing psych for PTSD. Every visit I would tell her about my CFS, joint pain and migraines. She was the one that actually got me the physical appointments I needed."

☐ **Veteran from Northampton, Pennsylvania** - "Have all the conditions mentioned, plus additionally shoulder pain from an injury in the service; tinnitus; lack of sleep .. Saw the same [VA] PCP for 10 years, who didn't really take my complaints seriously .. Now seeing new PCP; rheumatology; psychologist; & psychiatrist - and NOW they are seeing things that were ignored for years. Never told to 'see pysch' for pain, it was just patently ignored for years. .."

☐ **Veteran from Zanesville, Ohio** - "My issue has always been bad headaches that started in country in '91, right around the time the war started. I [go] to the Columbus Oh VA hospital and local CBOC. They always circle around and end up putting me on mental health meds that do nothing for the headaches and only cause negative side effects that are much worse than the headaches alone. After a year of being on them I took myself off for this very reason only to be put right back on them for the very same reason. They just think they gave me the wrong type! I feel like I gotta go thru the motion to prove they are not the solution. I keep telling them that it is my sinuses causing them right now and finally got an allergy Doctor to listen enough to put me on a round of antibiotics and within a week it helped enough that my headaches are so much better now that I do not have to take my pain meds. After dealing w/headaches for 25 years I feel the doctors need to listen to what we feel is causing it and what the solution may be because I feel I know my body better than a doctor who is seeing me for the first time."

☐ **Veteran from Oak Grove, Kentucky** - "I have been treated, well seen at the Nashville VA, since 1995 and have always been told "It's all in my head" and Somatoform disorder. I have all the classic problems, PTSD, Joint pain, back pain, pain in all joints except hips. CFS, anxiety, major depression, fibromyalgia, Migraines though the migraines have gotten a lot better in the past few years. .. Have also been seen at [several DOD and VA programs], All of which resulted in [VA] trying to validate that it was all psychological / Somatoform disorder."

☐ **Veteran from Cincinnati, Ohio** - "I was treated condescendingly at the Vet Center, got referred for psych help, and prescribed various drugs that only made things worse. Finally just quit trying, sucked it up, and just deal with it myself as best I can."

☐ **Veteran from Neola, Pennsylvania** - "I was almost immediately referred to Pysch. It has taken years, and a major decrease in my physical ability, to get anything more than the minimum health care. Fill me up with pills and move on. Pysch only set me up with pain management. So on one hand they admit pain but on the other they won't help."

☐ **Veteran from Hendersonville, Tennessee** - "Nashville V.A. Primary care doc prescribed me gabapentin for my joint pain, especially in my shoulders neck and knees. I still have extreme cramps in my legs and calves and some serious muscle spasms, not to mention how bad my hands shake. The fatigue, insomnia depression and anxiety my doc couldn't figure out so I was referred to the Shrinks."

☐ **Veteran from Cincinnati, Ohio** - "Since I already have a [psych] doc my physical problems are ignored."

☐ **Veteran from Fort Worth, Texas** - "I had a visit at the Fort Worth Clinic where they tried referring me to psych to "deal" with my pain but I basically cussed them out and shamed them then left for the Dallas VA only to be questioned as to whether I felt safe at home or not. It was a bad ordeal and they even put it in my records".

☐ **Veteran from Hampton, Virginia** - "..My husband asked my PCP if he knew anything about the Gulf War Illnesses and he bluntly said NO. Where did they find these doctors?"

☐ **Veteran from Parker, Colorado** - "My pcp is vaguely familiar with it; don't believe any [specialty doctors], GI, [for] example have any clue about GWI or that there was even a war fought. Let alone we are sick from it, Honestly I have a hard time bringing it up to any of them because of the look most of them give me when I have mentioned it to them, can't help to ask why can't there be some sort of flag like notice in med record that says something like "Vet is GWI Era possible or Confirmed GWI patient" then followed with instructions on how to proceed".

☐ **Veteran from Havelock, North Carolina** - "My VA pcp is truly a lost cause. None of the VA providers here in the VISN-6 region have [any] clue. Since moving here to NC from KY I have had 3 VA providers. None of which knew anything about the GWS."

☐ **Veteran from Dunnsville, Virginia** - "I have the same thing and they thought it was all in my mind at first but I kept complaining. As the time goes by the pain gets worse. I hurt and have a heart problem that they continuously ignore".
☐ **Veteran from London, England** - "this is happening in the UK as well."
☐ **Veteran from Denver, Colorado** - "I'm happy with my Denver VA provider. Treats the symptoms as best as he can and makes credible suggestions. Knowledgeable on GWI and doesn't sum it up as mental." -Veteran from southern Arizona - "You got lucky!"

CLAIMS ALSO AFFECTED. Not only are VA clinicians summarily dismissing the complaints of veterans suffering from extremely debilitating muscle pain, profound fatigue, chronic unexplained skin rashes, etc., VA seems to be following that exact same model for claims. For the veterans in this discussion group, it appears that if the veteran agrees to be seen by mental health professionals at the VA, it then seems like his or her chances of getting a disability claim approved are almost assured, whereas those who reject treatment by VA psychiatrists or psychologists seem more likely to have their claim denied. The following is a sampling of comments related to claims that various members of the Gulf War Illnesses Facebook page posted after I had asked the aforementioned question:

☐ **Veteran from Muskogee, Oklahoma** - ".. VA claims are easier for those claiming psychological (PTSD) issues but think it is bad for the veteran. If they have physical health conditions the doctors will minimize health issues because of the documented psychological problems and not do as many tests that may help them on down the road. .."
☐ **Veteran from Muscle Shoals, Alabama** - "When I received my letter denying my claim for stomach cancer the nurse that did the evaluation said my cancer was caused by SAD. Severe Anxiety Disorder. I have never been diagnosed by any Psychiatrist or psychologist???"
☐ **Veteran from Neosho, Missouri** - "I'm rated 90 percent with IU, but all my complaints and gulf war illnesses were denied individually and all was put under PTSD, filed claim at mount Vernon, Missouri and regional office St Louis, so yeah they did it wrong, but not going to rock the boat when I got total and permanent."
 fi **Veteran from Coatesville, Pennsylvania** - "Been seen for all and VA comes back and says not service related."
☐ **Veteran from Las Vegas, Nevada** - "Tomah VA treated both mental health and primary care until the OIG Investigation had them on Administrative Leave. Then nobody treated me until I filed a Congressional Complaint and spoke to Carolyn Clancy...Nothing got done still with referrals after their negligence. A few months later the PCP agreed to PTSD inpatient, but again stone-walled by their staff so it would look like my denial was my fault. I have all of the diagnosis and claim is still pending while now being referred in Las Vegas for numerous medical treatments. They don't acknowledge GWI here...then again they don't anywhere."
☐ **Veteran from Allegan, Michigan** - "In 1993 went to Los Angeles VA they pushed me through said nothing was wrong. In 2003 went to Phoenix VA same thing. In 2008 went to Sacramento VA was told I wasn't eligible for benefits. 2011 I was diagnosed by civilian Dr. with ulcerative colitis. 2013 had BCIR surgery by civilian Dr. 2014 registered at the Chicago VA never made an appointment because people are just plain mean there. In 2015 went to Wyoming Michigan VA. They have yet to do anything about my headaches, fatigue and joint pain, went through the shrink thing made them stop. 9 months later and I received 100% disability just for ulcerative colitis, 50% PTSD."
☐ **Veteran from Topeka, Kansas** - "I filed for undiagnosed illnesses of chronic fatigue and joint pain in 95. Denied for both but my VSO had added PTSD. (I was diagnosed with chronic fatigue and PTSD only at that time.) I have now managed to get a listing dx of CFS."
☐ **Veteran from Oak Grove, Kentucky** - "Only reason I kept going was because my claim was pending and if I didn't, they would say, I "refused treatment". Don't think any of my ratings are considered service connected or not. Afraid to mess with it as I'm getting .. [100% Individual Unemployability] so I'm leaving it alone for now."
☐ **Veteran from Eads, Tennessee** - "As soon as the VA read the words "stress" in my application for C& P for numerous ailments with unknown etiology from Desert Shield/Desert Storm I was sent to a psychologist at Memphis VA hospital for evaluation....you don't need to hear what he wrote....I felt betrayed and haven't been back since."

CONCLUSIONS

Gulf War Illness is a physiological illness, period. That's not just the opinion of this very ill veterans' advocate and multi-year CDMRP participant, it is the opinion of hundreds of Ph.D's and M.D.s who have studied Gulf War Illness over the past decade. These are highly skilled experts in the fields of science and medicine.

It's long past the time when the self-serving interests of political operatives and defense contractors trump the medical and financial needs of the more than 200,000 of America's 1991 Persian Gulf War veterans whose good health and ability to support their families is nothing more than a distant memory. This American tragedy must be brought to end, once and for all. History is watching, and everyone involved will be judged according to his or her actions, or inaction. Which side of history will you be on?

Very Respectfully Submitted,

David Keith Winnett, Jr.
Captain, United States Marine Corps (Retired)
Representing: Veterans for Common Sense
Home address: New Braunfels, Texas

LEA STEELE, PH.D.

Yudofsky Chair in Behavioral Neuroscience, Professor of Neuropsychiatry
Baylor College of Medicine

My name is Dr. Lea Steele. I am a neuroepidemiologist and have conducted research on the health of Gulf War veterans since the late 1990s. Our initial efforts were sponsored by the State of Kansas, where we worked with state officials to establish a research and outreach program for Persian Gulf War veterans in Kansas, collaborating with Kansas State University. Since those early years I have continued clinical and population research on Gulf War health issues and have served on multiple federal Gulf War research panels, including 5 years as Scientific Director of the Congressionally-mandated Research Advisory Committee on Gulf War Veterans' Illnesses. I am currently a professor at Baylor College of Medicine in Houston, where our veterans' health research continues.

I am submitting this statement to offer my perspective, as an experienced Gulf War scientist, on where things stand with federal efforts to address health outcomes in 1991 Gulf War veterans, 25 years after Desert Storm. With respect to Gulf War illness (GWI), the signature health problem of the 1991 Gulf War, we have seen significant progress in understanding its nature and its causes, and the magnitude of the problem. We can diagnose GWI by its consistent profile of symptoms that have now persisted, for many veterans, for 25 years. Symptoms include chronic headaches, widespread pain, debilitating fatigue, cognitive difficulties and other concurrent problems. We know GWI affects a substantial proportion of the nearly 700,000 veterans who served in Desert Storm-roughly 25–30%. We know GWI is not a psychiatric disorder and was not caused by combat or stress-PTSD rates are relatively low in Gulf War veterans, as expected from the four day ground war in which most personnel did not see combat. Rather, research has most consistently pointed to chemical exposures widely encountered by veterans during deployment-toxicants that, individually and in combination, have long-term adverse effects on the brain and other systems.

I want to emphasize just how consequential this scientific progress has been, and the promise it offers for understanding GWI, for avoiding this problem in future deployments, and for near-term identification of diagnostic tests and treatments for veterans who have suffered for so long.

Gulf War illness is a complex disorder that was long denied or minimized by federal agencies charged with addressing it. The fact that we have learned so much about the nature and causes of GWI, especially in the last 10 years, is the result of several important factors: the persistence and dedication of Gulf War veterans who have continued to push federal agencies to find answers and treatments, the persistence of Congress in directing that government agencies provide the needed research, healthcare, and benefits, and the diligent work of dedicated scientists.

Still, despite impressive progress, the most essential work remains. That work is to ensure that the large number of veterans who still suffer from the long term medical consequences of service in the 1991 Gulf War are diagnosed and effectively treated. This effort is underway, and scientists working in this arena are now seeing returns in the push to better understand the biology of GWI and identify treatments that significantly improve the health of Gulf War veterans. This is exemplified by the rapid expansion of treatment studies-both in ill Gulf War veterans and animal models of Gulf War illness-sponsored in recent years by the DOD's Office of Congressionally Directed Medical Research Programs (CDMRP).

While the DOD, researchers, and veterans have made important strides in understanding and addressing this serious problem, VA has lagged behind in providing an effective response to Gulf War health issues. The poor response was more understandable in the early years after the Gulf War, when little was understood about this problem. But it continues today, reflected day in day out in the difficulties Gulf War veterans face in obtaining effective care at VA. These pervasive problems are also evident in the Clinical Practice Guidelines issued in 2014 to inform VA healthcare providers about treatment options for veterans with Gulf War illness. They are evident in the lack of the fundamental VA research necessary to inform IOM panels and the Secretary of Veterans Affairs concerning benefits decisions. And they are evident in ill-informed findings resulting from a piecemeal approach to the evidence considered in a recent IOM report commissioned and charged by VA.

With regard to the recent treatment guidelines and IOM report, a long list of specific examples could be provided that illustrate the limitations, misassumptions, and errors contained in these documents. For those experienced in conducting research and caring for ill Gulf War veterans, these reports are the latest in a long line of clinical and research missteps from VA. In many ways, they harken back to the 1990s, before the now extensive evidence was available to inform our understanding of GWI, and guide the steps required to effectively address it.

For example, the recent IOM report states that Gulf War illness studies have largely excluded psychological problems and recommends that future efforts incorporate mind-body approaches to this problem. In fact, the opposite is true. Gulf War studies have always included psychological issues and, until recent years, focused more heavily on psychological factors than any other single area. Research consistently found no association between combat stress and GWI, and studies found little effect of behavioral therapies in improving veterans' symptoms. Today, stress is no longer the central focus of GWI research. But studies continue to evaluate psychological symptoms and psychiatric comorbidities in Gulf War veterans, and treatment studies are testing mind-body therapeutic interventions to alleviate veterans' symptoms. To suggest an increased emphasis on psychological factors and interventions is baffling and misrepresents widely available evidence.

Similarly, the 2014 Clinical Practice Guidelines for VA healthcare providers emphasize the use of psychiatric medications and behavioral interventions, despite there being no evidence that these treatments provide meaningful benefit for veterans with GWI. Studies, again, have demonstrated just the opposite, that behavioral interventions provide little benefit for veterans with GWI. Proceeding in the direction suggested by just these two examples would misdirect precious resources and, more importantly, further delay the appropriate medical care needed by veterans.

From my perspective as a scientist, there are two common threads that have undermined the effectiveness of VA programs to effectively address GWI. (1) VA's ongoing failure to affirmatively engage GWI as a medical condition that affects veterans as a result of their deployment to the Kuwaiti Theater of Operations in 1990–1991. The most fundamental essentials are lacking. VA still does not refer to this condition by an identifiable name and VA clinicians have few resources and little training in how best to assist veterans with this condition. (2) VA's failure to bring in experts to develop and steer healthcare and research programs that effectively address Gulf War health issues. Gulf War illness is a complex and unfamiliar medical condition, and effective VA programs require scientific and clinical expertise specific to this problem. In contrast to VA, the scientific progress brought about by DOD's effective Gulf War Illness Research Program in recent years can be traced directly to DOD's developing this program in partnership with scientific experts who are most experienced in Gulf War research and Gulf War veterans who are most affected by this problem.

It goes without saying that Gulf War veterans deserve clear answers, effective healthcare, and informed research to improve their health. It is a travesty that, 25 years after the brief war and heroic victory achieved by the military in Operation Desert Storm, veterans who served in that war continue to have to fight for recognition, care, and benefits for the long-term health problems they still suffer as a consequence of their service.

Questions For The Record

Questions from Chairman Mike Coffman for the Department of Veterans Affairs:

Question 1: According to the 2013 report of the Institute of Medicine (IOM), studies referenced were from 2008 and earlier and provided a disclaimer that drug manufacturers may have influenced several clinical trials or employed researchers. VA used those same studies in writing its guidelines. Was VA aware of the potential that its guidelines are based on questionable material?

VA Response: Yes, VA was aware of such concerns. VA and the Department of Defense (DoD) have a rigorous process for assessing and rating the quality of published studies used in the development of our joint Clinical Practice Guidelines (CPGs). More specifically, this process was used in the development of the DoD/VA Chronic Multi-Symptom Illness Clinical Practice Guideline.

Question 2: That same IOM report noted a high risk of bias for a number of studies that are also referenced as sources for VA's treatment of Gulf War Veterans. Was VA aware of this when it used them to create the guidelines?

VA Response: Yes, as mentioned above, VA was aware of such concerns and addressed them in the process of development of DoD/VA CPGs through a process of rating the strength and quality of various studies being considered.

Questions 3: Since VA wrote the contract that employed IOM for the study, why didn't VA exclude questionable or high risk material in the study or do so in the results the department continued to tout?

VA Response: Because scientific and clinical evidence exists on a spectrum of strength and quality, VA, IOM, DoD and similar organizations, as well as scientific researchers evaluate the "strengths and limitations" of studies and research based evidence. That is the approach used in the interpretation of IOM reports as well as in the development of DoD/VA CPGs.

Question 4: VA's guidelines state "an internal working document" of VHA and DOD was used in developing the guidelines. Please provide that document in its entirety.

VA RESPONSE: The "internal working document" identified in the request is the "Guideline for Guidelines" which can be accessed directly at http://www.healthquality.va.gov/documents/cpgGuidelinesForGuidelinesFinalRevisions051214.docx.

This document outlines the process from start to finish for the development of VA/DoD CPGs. It covers such areas as: identifying and requesting a VA/DoD CPG be developed, identifying subject matter experts from both VA and DoD agencies, methodology for key question development and evidence review, evidence grading, potential conflict of interest, adapting/adopting/new CPG development, internal/external review and approval process.

QUESTION 5: IT HAS BEEN FORTY YEARS SINCE THE VIETNAM WAR ENDED AND VETERANS HAD TO FIGHT FOR CARE RELATED TO AGENT ORANGE. IT HAS BEEN TWENTY-FIVE YEARS SINCE THE PERSIAN GULF WAR, AND VETERANS ARE STILL FIGHTING FOR THEIR CARE. NOW, VETERANS ARE ALSO DEALING WITH BURN PITS AND OTHER TOXIC RELATED ISSUES. IS VA GETTING THE OCCUPATIONAL AND ENVIRONMENTAL HEALTH SURVEILLANCE DATA THAT IT NEEDS FROM DOD IN ORDER TO CARE FOR VETERANS PROPERLY? IF NOT, WHAT ADDITIONAL DATA WOULD BE HELPFUL AND WHY?

VA RESPONSE: Unfortunately, for many Veterans, particularly those of the Vietnam and the Persian Gulf Wars, it appears that reliable occupational and environmental health surveillance data just do not exist. To the extent that such data are available, DoD shares them with VA as needed. DoD has much better surveillance data available for more recent conflicts and events.

Building on the lessons learned from the Persian Gulf War, Operation Enduring Freedom (OEF), Operation Iraqi Freedom (OIF), and Operation New Dawn (OND), VA and DoD work collaboratively to identify and measure military related exposures, to identify those potentially exposed, and to generate risk estimates for any known or potential acute and long term health effects.

The evolution of the Agent Orange benefits program is an excellent example of the progress VA has made in terms of support for individuals with deployment related environmental exposures. It is an extremely "worker friendly policy" for those whose health may have been negatively impacted by dioxin exposure in the places and time periods designated. The Airborne Hazards and Open Burn Pit Registry is also a measure of how much more proactively we are approaching the documentation, assessment, and monitoring of deployment related exposure concerns. http://www.va.gov/HEALTH/NewsFeatures/2016/March/Were-you-exposed-to-burn-pits-while-deployed.asp.

The Tomodachi Registry of about 75,000 DoD-affiliated individuals (Service members, family members, veterans, contractors) in the vicinity of Japanese Dai-ichi reactor meltdown was created and populated immediately after the disaster and includes individual- and geolocation-sampling readings of ionizing radiation exposure levels. This registry could prove very useful in the future, as needs arise for potential future follow-up in the overall health of this Veteran population.

A major emphasis of the DoD/VA Deployment Health Work Group (DHWG) is on Service members returning from OEF, OIF, or OND. The DHWG also coordinates initiatives related to Veterans of all eras. Joint efforts continue to increase sharing of health surveillance information and review of relevant literature on hazardous environmental exposures, so that risky situations in theater are identified, and the Department's responses are appropriately coordinated. The DHWG analyzed complex clinical medicine, toxicology, and policy aspects to develop synchronized DoD and VA actions. The DHWG organized twelve meetings in FY15 to coordinate DoD and VA responses to five major environmental exposures in Iraq, Afghanistan, and the US, as described below:

- potential health effects of exposure to burn pit smoke in OEF/OIF/OND
- potential health effects of high ambient concentrations of particulate matter in OEF/OIF/OND
- potential health effects of chemical warfare agent exposure in OIF
- potential health effects of historical exposure to contaminated drinking water at Marine Corps Base Camp Lejeune, NC
- potential health effects of exposure to Agent Orange during and after the Vietnam War

The DHWG provides ongoing oversight of the development of the Individual Longitudinal Exposure Record (ILER) project, including briefings every two months. The goal of ILER is to create a complete record of every Service member's occupational and environmental exposures over the course of their career. ILER is a $19.1 million jointly funded pilot project and the goals are: to demonstrate the feasibility of producing ILER; and to develop a prototype that provides an initial operating capacity (IOC). At IOC, DoD and VA will decide whether to proceed to Full Operating Capability, which would require considerable sustainment funding from both Departments in future years.

The ILER will mine several existing DoD data systems that contain in-garrison and deployment exposure-related information. It will link career location and year with exposure data and will be available to DoD and VA health care providers to help inform diagnosis and treatment, and to VBA claims adjudicators to help establish service connection. This will assist Veterans in establishing their individual exposures.

Question 6: In 2015, GAO reported that DOD provided VA with access to unclassified summaries of historical environmental health surveillance monitoring efforts through a website. The summaries are referred to as POEMS (or Periodic Occupational and Environmental Monitoring Summaries). However, VA officials were uncertain about how often these summaries were being used. Is VA using these summaries, and if so, how often and to what extent?

VA Response: Clinicians at the War Related Illness and Injury Study Centers (WRIISCs) perform specialty consultations about the environmental and occupational health and exposure concerns of Veterans referred for evaluation. They use their expertise to regularly incorporate information from the POEMs and the online information request services available from the Army Public Health Center, as well as personal contacts at the Army Public Health Center and the Navy and Marine Corps Public Health Center to complete their assessments and recommendations. The services of Army Public Health Center are available to any clinician or patient according to their website, but are perhaps most suitable to specialty evaluations.

Here is the website for the Army Public Health Center. More detail is available here under the "topics and services" and "request services" tabs. https://phc.amedd.army.mil/Pages/default.aspx.

Question 7: How does VA use DOD's occupational and environmental health surveillance data? Does it play a role in how VA treats patients with Gulf War Illnesses? If so, please explain in detail.

VA Response: DoD's occupational and environmental health surveillance data are used in accordance with its completeness, accuracy, and relevance to help address the health concerns reported by Veterans. The DoD has provided tremendous support in the development of an Airborne Hazards and Open Burn Pit Registry by providing data for pre-population of deployment dates and locations using information from existing DoD databases. Earlier efforts to construct a model of the plume of low-dose chemical warfare agent dispersion from the Kamisiyah demolition have been subject to criticism by GAO and IOM, but used the best data and methodologies available at the time to understand the exposure. Treatment decisions are handled based on clinical presentation of the individual patient, including the Veteran's self-reported history of exposures and the scientific soundness and safety of available therapy options.

In the routine care of Veterans, clinicians are encouraged to ask Veterans about their military experience, and in the case of specialized assessments, utilize principles of occupational medicine and knowledge about known hazards to reconstruct a self-reported exposure assessment. This can then be used by clinicians to estimate the extent of their patients' possible exposure to such hazards and to develop a crude probability of any known or possible long term health effects related to these exposure(s). The treating providers then continue to monitor these patients for any possible associated condition(s) that may clinically manifest as a result of their in-service exposure to such hazards. It is important to recognize that clinicians will also treat patients with known or suspected exposures in a holistic and caring matter.

Question 8: IOM Volume 8 noted a fifteen percent excess of lung cancer for Gulf War Veterans and recommended further follow up because "cancer incidence in the past 10 years has not been reported." Yet, IOM Volume 10 mentions a lack of sufficient evidence between deployment to the Gulf War and any form of cancer. Please provide the updated disease specific incidence and mortality data accounting for this change.

VA Response: The IOM Volume 10 does not have readily available disease specific cancer mortality that would compare deployed and non-deployed populations. The IOM however used several studies to study cancer incidence. A recent study of Australian Veterans showed no definitive difference in deployed versus non-deployed Veterans for any cancer except for a statistically significant increase in thyroid cancer based on five events. (Sim et al., 2015)[1] A large scale second study looked at Veterans diagnosed with cancer using data from the Defense Manpower Data Center, which was linked to central cancer registries in 28 states and to the VA Central Cancer Registry. Using statistical methods that included regression analyses, lung cancer was the only site-specific cancer found to have a significantly higher proportion among deployed Veterans compared with non-deployed era Veterans (PIR = 1.15, 95 percent CI 1.03–1.29). [Note: this appears to be the 15 percent increase cited above and is found in Volume 10] However, the risk was not increased over the general population. An important caveat is that smoking history, the known primary cause of lung cancer, was not controlled for in the study. Other cancers did not show an elevation of risk. Overall, after controlling for age, race, and sex, there was no significant association between Gulf status and the proportion of Veterans with a cancer (odds ratio, 0.99; 95 percent CI, 0.96–1.02) identified from a state registry. (Young et al., 2010).[2]

It is important to recognize, however, as the IOM Volume 10 states: the length of follow-up was, at most, 15 years, which may not be enough time for certain cancers such as lung cancer to develop if there were a Gulf War exposure factor. A

---

[1] Sim, M., D. Clarke, B. Forbes, D. Glass, S. Gwini, J. Ikin, H. Kelsall, D. McKenzie, B. Wright, A. McFarlane, M. Creamer, and K. Horsley. 2015. Australian Gulf War Veterans' follow up health study: Technical report 2015. Canberra, Australia: Department of Veterans' Affairs.

[2] Young, H. A., J. D. Maillard, P. H. Levine, S. J. Simmens, C. M. Mahan, and H. K. Kang. 2010. Investigating the risk of cancer in 1990–1991 U.S. Gulf War Veterans with the use of state cancer registry data. Annals of Epidemiology 20(4):265–272.

study led by VA (Dursa et. al., 2016)[3] used survey data of thousands of Veterans and demonstrated no statistical increase in cancers, but brain cancer was slightly elevated at 1.02 OR. Finally, VA provided a health care use report for Gulf War era deployed and non-deployed Veterans who sought care in VA facilities from October 2001 to December 2013. These VA health care users represent 46 percent of all deployed Gulf War Veterans and 36 percent of all non-deployed era Veterans. This data also has deployed Veterans with a slightly lower percentage of lung or trachea cancers (6.0 percent versus. 6.3 percent) out of all cancers diagnoses than non-deployed Veterans. Importantly, an ongoing VA technical workgroup, which includes VA, will look closely at all available data/cited publications on all cancers, and especially, review the results for lung cancer for its upcoming technical workgroup report and recommendations to the Secretary.

Question 9: Given the O&I hearing in June 2015, where videos of VA employees acknowledged that the department is making drug addicts out of Veterans and the CDC and American Medical Association's concerns related to overmedication were highlighted, why is VA prescribing these serious drugs for Gulf War Illness?

VA Response: Some of the drug categories of concern due to their potential to cause addiction and/or unintentional overdose (or other adverse outcomes) are opioid medications, benzodiazepines (medications for sleep and anxiety), stimulants, immunotherapies, antibiotics and corticosteroids. These are specifically mentioned as medications to avoid as treatments for Gulf War Illness (GWI) related CMI in Veterans unless clinically indicated for co-occurring conditions With respect to opioids in particular, the guideline states "Avoid the long-term use of opioid medications" unless clinically indicated. In general, the CPG suggests that treatment teams "Maximize the use of non-pharmacologic therapies".

Question 10: In its 2011 report, the IOM recommended that additional studies of health effects in Veterans deployed to Iraq and Afghanistan were needed to help determine whether certain long-term health effects were likely to result from exposure to burn pits during deployments. Please describe the research VA conducted in response to this recommendation.

VA Response: VA and DoD research on respiratory illness among Veterans deployed to Iraq and Afghanistan is focused on: (1) determining the prevalence and severity of lung disease associated with deployment to South West Asia, (SWA) and, (2) identifying the geographical, behavioral, medical, and causative factors related to deployment associated lung disease.

In 2013, VA's East Orange, New Jersey WRIISC launched the Airborne Hazards Center of Excellence to provide comprehensive medical evaluations focused on the respiratory health in deployed Veterans. Their clinical research has addressed several important gaps in the diagnostic evaluation of symptomatic Veterans, in addition to addressing Veterans' health concerns through direct patient care. Their research efforts have resulted in 12 peer-reviewed publications, eight conference abstracts, and a book chapter. East Orange WRIISC researchers reviewed data published from 2001 to 2014 pertaining to respiratory health in military personnel deployed to Iraq and/or Afghanistan and found 19 unique studies. In summary, published data based on case reports and retrospective cohort studies suggest a higher prevalence of respiratory symptoms and respiratory illness in Veterans deployed to Iraq and/or Afghanistan. However, the association between chronic lung disease and airborne hazards exposure requires further longitudinal research studies with objective pulmonary assessments.

VA's Office of Research and Development (ORD) funds research projects that address respiratory health issues in Veterans deployed to Iraq and Afghanistan. ORD's Request for Applications under the "Merit Review Award for Deployment Health Research OEF/OIF/OND" lists the health effects of burn pits as a specific area of emphasis.

ORD funded research projects completed in 2015:

- Effects of Deployment Exposures on Cardiopulmonary and Autonomic Function; Investigator: Michael Falvo, PhD; East Orange, New Jersey
- Nanoparticle Coupled Antioxidants for Respiratory Illness in Veterans; Investigator: Rodney Schlosser, MD; Charleston, Sout Carolina

[3] Dursa, E. K., S. K. Barth, A. I. Schneiderman, and R. M. Bossarte. 2016. Physical and mental health status of Gulf War and Gulf era Veterans. Journal of Occupational and Environmental Medicine 58(1):41–46.

Ongoing ORD funded research:

- Mechanisms of Cigarette Smoke-Induced Acute Lung Injury; Investigator: Sharon Rounds, MD; Providence, Rhode Island (7/1/2015–6/30/2019)
- Carbon Black Induced Activation of Lung Antigen-Presenting Cells (APCs); Investigator: David B. Corry, MD; Houston, Texas (7/1/2013–6/30/2017)
- Targeting HSC-derived Circulating Fibroblast Precursors in Pulmonary Fibrosis; Investigator: Amanda C. LaRue, PhD; Charleston, South Carolina

(10/1/2013–9/30/2017).

VA continues to make use of longitudinal research studies to evaluate the respiratory health of deployed Veterans. VA and DoD have developed an Interagency Agreement to support the joint examination of data collected by the Millennium Cohort Study. The aim of this collaboration is to evaluate the impact of military service on health and disease over time.

The VA-led National Health Study of a New Generation of US Veterans sampled 60,000 OEF/OIF deployed Service members and non-deployed Veterans in 2008, and administered a survey that included self-reported measures of exposure and disease. The New Generation study has resulted in one publication analyzing prevalence of respiratory diseases, and additional analyses are underway.

In addition, VA conducts ongoing surveillance of VA health care utilization through systematic reviews and investigation of diseases treated. This surveillance drives in-depth investigation of areas of special concern, such as respiratory diseases. These studies enable VA to identify potential adverse health effects associated with deployment, including respiratory disease, and follow them over time.

Question 11: On February 11th, VA issued its final report on Gulf War Illness, which had similar findings to IOM's previous report. IOM concluded that future research efforts need to focus on the interconnectedness of the brain and the rest of the body's organ systems when seeking to improve treatment of Veterans for Gulf War Illness. What actions, if any, does VA plan to take in response to this report?

VA Response: VA has implemented a technical workgroup (see VA Response for Question 16 for details) to review all the recommendations in this report and to provide recommendations in response to the report to the Secretary of Veterans Affairs. This will include a review of this important recommendation. VA also plans to have listening sessions in the near future with Veterans to get their input into this and other IOM recommendations, as well as getting that of the Research Advisory Committee on Gulf War Veterans' Illnesses. The VA takes seriously the idea that ongoing research will need to focus on the holistic treatment of Veterans; as such, VA research will aim to find solutions that take into account the inter-connectedness of the brain with other organ systems.

One area where VA is increasing its focus is Integrative Health Care (IHC). Still, we caution that positive research findings related to use of IHC do not automatically translate into available clinical services, because VA may only provide care that is in accord with generally accepted standards of medical practice and is needed to promote, preserve, or restore health as provided in 38 Code of Federal Regulations 17.38(b). To this end, VA is conducting a randomized control trial, entitled "Complementary and Alternative Medicine (CAM) for Sleep, Health Functioning, and Quality of Life in Veterans with Gulf War (GW) Veterans' Illnesses"," also referred to as the GW–CAM Study. This study examines Gulf War Veterans Illness by assessing the hallmark conditions of pain, fatigue, sleep and cognitive difficulty, and the efficacy of a CAM intervention on these conditions. To further expand our understanding of Gulf War Veterans Illness and the efficacy of a CAM treatment intervention, the GW–CAM Study has also partnered with the Department of Defense to develop a brain imaging protocol that will be incorporated into the GW–CAM Study.

Question 12: Dr. Hunt's testimony was that psychiatric medications should not be given for Gulf War Illness and yet the clinical guidelines created and promulgated by VA (including Dr. Hunt) recommending numerous pharmacologic agents for Gulf War Illness. Please explain this discrepancy in detail.

VA Response: The Chronic Multi-Symptom Illness (CMI) CPG is based upon current evidence-based approaches to CMI. The specific symptoms experienced by Gulf War Veterans vary from one Veteran to another. Given that treatment for CMI/Gulf War Illness is primarily aimed at symptom management, the treatment approaches are personalized and will vary from Veteran to Veteran, depending upon whether an individual has fatigue, pain, cognitive disturbances, gastrointestinal disorders or other symptoms as their predominant manifestation of CMI.

Certain medications that are also used for depression, such as selective serotonin reuptake inhibitors and serotonin-norepinephrine reuptake inhibitors (SNRI's) have also been found to be helpful in symptom reduction in individuals with pain-predominant CMI, fatigue predominant CMI or global symptoms CMI. These medications, when clinically appropriate and used in the care of Gulf War Veterans are not being used as "psychiatric medications". They are being used to offer relief from specific symptoms or combinations of symptoms. In general, the CPG advocates treatment teams to "Maximize the use of non-pharmacologic therapies" as clinically appropriate; again, our providers must abide by the applicable standards of care and these may involve the use of certain drugs in a particular patient case, especially where the use of non-pharmacologic therapies has not been effective.

Question 13: Dr. Hunt's presentation titled "A Model for Providing Services for Returning Combat Veterans," implies that he and others in VA believe Gulf War Illness is a "mental disorder." This is further substantiated in Dr. Hunt's Community of Practice call conducted Friday, March 11th. During this call, VA discussed issues related to our subcommittee's hearing held on February 23rd. The call included more than fifty participants, and it discussed how to improve care for Veterans suffering from Gulf War Illness. Unfortunately, the majority of the attention was given to a presentation by Dr. David Kearney regarding chronic pain, with what seemed to be an emphasis on PTSD - and the use of mindfulness as a method of treatment for Gulf War Illness. Please explain in detail the discrepancy in Dr. Hunt's public statements and his internal VA discussions and presentations.

VA Response: Dr. Hunt's presentation, "A Model for Providing Services for Returning Combat Veterans," was not intended to imply that he and others in VA believe Gulf War Illness is a "mental disorder." The presentation focuses on the importance of understanding and responding effectively to the complex experience of combat. Environmental exposures are one aspect of that experience, and a particularly important aspect in our Gulf War Veterans as is pointed out in slides 25 - 32 presented to the Committee. This is important whether considering entitlement to benefits administered by VHA or VBA. The importance of assisting Veterans in accessing benefits is mentioned in several slides that were presented.

Question 14: Does Dr. Hunt believe Gulf War Illness is specifically a mental, psychiatric, psychologic, or psychosomatic issue? Please do not convolute the answer by discussing the obvious mind-body connection associated with how the brain works in relation to body mechanics.

VA Response: No. As Dr. Hunt stated in his testimony, he does not believe that Gulf War illness is specifically a mental, psychiatric, psychological, or psychosomatic issue. Dr. Hunt's board certification is in Occupational and Environmental medicine, the medical specialty that focuses on toxic exposures in the home, workplace, and other external environments. He is a Clinical Associate Professor in this program at the University of Washington. From the beginning, his work with Gulf War Veterans has been oriented primarily towards ensuring that they receive the care that will most effectively support them.

He has admittedly been very concerned that at times the debate over "what causes Gulf War Illness" (a challenging, but nonetheless extremely important, question that still has not been answered after 25 years of research) has distracted both the clinical and research communities from offering effective support for these Veterans. He does not question the fact that environmental exposures have contributed to the health concerns of GW Veterans and consistently promotes two important parallel courses of action:

1.Ongoing research to identify specific causal relationships between specific exposures (or combinations of exposures) and health conditions in GW Veterans so that specific targeted treatments can be established (such as CoQ10 which he mentioned in his testimony); and,

2.Until such relationships and targeted treatments are clearly established, clinicians must provide effective condition-specific treatment. General and specialist health care is available under VA's medical benefits package to enrolled Veterans to ensure they do well. VA's treatment authority for GW Veterans is broadly worded and permits VA to treat them at no cost for conditions that may be associated with their service in the Gulf War; not withstanding the current lack of evidence that such a condition (s) is associated with such service. Only those conditions that can be ruled out by the USH as not being associated with such service are excluded and those are few in number.

Quesiton 15: Many Veterans have complained that VA's questionnaires to Veterans suffering from Gulf War Illness (GWI) are worded in such a way to reach a preconceived finding that GWI is a mental issue or a PTSD issue. Please submit all such questionnaires provided to Veterans and all responses from the recipients of the questionnaire.

VA Response: VA has conducted a number of research studies on the health concerns of Gulf War Veterans. The largest study has followed the same panel of 30,000 Gulf War Era Veterans with three surveys since 1995; half of the Veterans selected for the study deployed to the Gulf and the other half served elsewhere. The goal of this study was to assess the health of Gulf War and Gulf War Era Veterans. Each of three surveys administered over this period has asked a core set of questions important for assessing major domains of well-being, illness, and health determinants, or risk factors. Health has many domains: physical, mental, reproductive, functional, and social. This study completed its most recent follow up assessment in 2012 was a comprehensive assessment of multiple domains of health among Gulf War and Gulf War Era Veterans. While certain health conditions may be more prevalent among Gulf War Veterans, the purpose of this study is not to focus on one particular domain or health condition, but to present a population level assessment of the health of Gulf War and Gulf War Era Veterans.

This will help VA better understand any possible associations between their service and the clinical symptoms, and so better serve this population of Veterans. The questionnaire included standard validated scales and screening tools that are used widely both in clinical practice and in research. The inclusion of questions that measure symptoms of PTSD and other mental health conditions is based on evidence from the peer-reviewed literature that demonstrates these conditions are prevalent among Veterans (regardless of era or deployment status) and are associated with poor health outcomes overall. The principles of good questionnaire design dictate the selection of validated scales, construction of clear questions, and layout choices that elicits information in an unbiased fashion; the questionnaires used to study this panel of Gulf War Era Veterans have not been worded in such a way as to reach a preconceived result regarding the etiology of GWI or any association it may have with mental health symptoms or PTSD. This study has consistently provided evidence that Gulf War Veterans who deployed are sicker than their non-deployed peers. Notably, this study provided early evidence to support the understanding of Gulf War Illnesses as a multisystem illness state.

Copies of the IRB and OMB-approved surveys that were sent to Veteran participants of this study in 1995, 2005, and 2012 are attached. VA cannot provide all responses from the recipients of the questionnaires; as the research participants did not consent to have their individual data shared.

Question 16: Given VA's public acknowledgement that Gulf War Illness is a biological disorder, please explain why VA's clinical treatment protocols treat it as a psychological disorder.

VA Response: The DoD/VA CMI CPG does not treat GWI as a psychological disorder. It can be found on the web page of the DoD/VA Clinical Practice Guidelines in the section of "Military Related." It is not included in the section of the website where DoD/VA's related CPGs to mental health are found. http://www.healthquality.va.gov/. This underscores that it is considered to be a deployment health matter. The CPG is meant to offer guidance in how to provide effective care for Veterans with CMI. It begins by advocating that each Veteran be assigned a basic medical team "including a behavioral health specialist in Primary Care." This is standard for all Veterans enrolled in VA's health care system, particularly those who have been deployed to combat theaters. "Deployment related exposures" are one of a number of "critical domains" for knowledge on these teams. The standard of care in VA is to have behavioral health available for any Veteran who needs it through their expanded Patient Aligned Care Team.

Question 17: What is VA's opinion of IOM's conclusions in its most recent report given the similarities with its last report? Is VA satisfied that sufficient progress is being made to identify and better understand the causes of Gulf War Illness?

VA Response: A technical workgroup (TWG) of VA subject matter experts has been assembled to review IOM's report, Gulf War and Health: Volume 10: Update of Health Effects of Serving in the Gulf War, 2016. This TWG is working to determine how the findings and recommendations might help to identify possible adverse health effects related to such service in order to make a recommendation to the VA Secretary as to whether to establish a presumption of service-connection for a certain condition(s). This review will also include all other information and peer-reviewed literature which have become recently available. The TWG will draft a formal VA response document with recommended courses of action which will then be carefully staffed through senior leadership. Ultimately, the recommendations will go to the Secretary of Veterans Affairs for decision. This process is expected to take 3 - 4 months. VA would be happy to discuss our ongoing process in this regard, but feel that it is presently premature to discuss our impressions or views.

Question 18: What is VA's opinion of IOM's decision not to consider the results of animal research in its conclusions?

VA Response: The IOM committee conducted an extensive review of animal research related to Gulf War Veterans' symptoms. VA will be discussing in its technical workgroup (see above) the results of the animal studies and the ways in which these studies were evaluated and used by the IOM committee in drawing their conclusions. The IOM recommendations about possible future research concerning the validity of animal models will also be considered by the TWG, but it would be premature to make comments about specific IOM conclusions and recommendations before the work of VA's TWG is complete.

Question 19: What is VA's opinion of the Research Advisory Committee (RAC) on Gulf War Veterans' Illnesses (RAC)'s 2008 report, which used animal studies to conclude that pyridostigmine bromide pills and pesticide are associated with War Illness?

VA Response: In its 2008 report (http://www.va.gov/RAC- GWVI/docs/Committee—Documents/GWIandHealthofGWVeterans—RAC- GWVIReport—2008.pdf), the RAC on Gulf War Veterans' Illnesses concluded that there was "strong support for both PB [pyridostigmine bromide] and pesticides as causal factors in Gulf War illness." (p. 185).

In its report, Gulf War and Health: Volume 8 (2010), (http://www.nap.edu/catalog/12835/gulf-war-and-health-volume-8-update-of-health-effects), IOM reviewed the publications cited by the RAC and determined that there was "insufficient support for the conclusion" reached by the RAC (p. 279). The IOM indicated that there was a lack of association in agricultural workers who used pesticides regularly, a lack of persistent effects on the central nervous systems in animals, and a lack of consistent results in studies of Gulf War Veterans.

VA's position, based on IOM's earlier reports (excluding Volume 10 published in 2016) is that the cause of Gulf War illness is not yet known with certainty, even though groups of qualified scientists and physicians have reviewed the same data, including animal studies.

Question 20: Please explain the reasons for the turnover in leadership and membership of the RAC that has occurred since 2013. As part of your response, please provide the background and qualifications for each of the current committee members.

VA Response: This committee, required by section 104(b) of Public Law 105–368 (1998), is, in addition to relevant VA policy, subject to the Federal Advisory Committee Act (FACA), codified at 5 U.S.C. App., and regulations administered by the General Services Administration.

As a committee governed by the FACA, the RAC is required to follow FACA guidelines and VA policy. The charter (http://www.va.gov/RAC–GWVI/docs/Committee—Documents/CharterRACGWVI2015May.pdf) for the RAC specifies that the Chair can be appointed for an initial 2— year term and may be reappointed for an additional 1 or 2-year term. Similarly, the remaining members can be appointed for a 2 or 3 - year term and may be reappointed for an additional 1 or 2 - year term. As of 2013, six members had served since the committee was formed in 2002, three had served since 2005, and one each had served since 2006, 2007, and 2008. To become compliant with FACA and VA policy, approximately one-third of the committee members were to be replaced in each of the next three years. Membership rotations will continue each year into the future to ensure that multiple viewpoints from scientists, physicians, and Veterans are brought to VA. Nominations for membership are solicited in the Federal Registry. Brief biographies of current members are available on the RAC webpage (http://www.va.gov/RAC–GWVI/Members—and—Consultants.asp).